Provocations for Learning
in Early Years Settings

PROVOCATIONS for LEARNING in EARLY YEARS SETTINGS

A PRACTICAL GUIDE

Margaret Longstaffe

Jessica Kingsley Publishers
London and Philadelphia

First published in 2020
by Jessica Kingsley Publishers
73 Collier Street
London N1 9BE, UK
and
400 Market Street, Suite 400
Philadelphia, PA 19106, USA

www.jkp.com

Library of Congress Cataloging in Publication Data
A CIP catalog record for this book is available from the Library of Congress

British Library Cataloguing in Publication Data
A CIP catalogue record for this book is available from the British Library

ISBN 978 1 78592 495 8
eISBN 978 1 78450 882 1

Printed and bound in Great Britain

Contents

To Start at the Very Beginning, It's a Very Good Place to Start...

When I was a book-obsessed five-year-old my favourite way to spend a Saturday morning was to spend as long as humanly possible in a tiny little bookshop that was to be found around the corner from my house. I looked forward to Saturday morning all week, and as the days passed I would silently cross them off in my mind, waiting for Saturday morning to arrive. I would then spend the first part of the morning asking if it was time to go to the bookshop! Luckily for me my dad was equally obsessed with reading and books (thanks Dad), and if we didn't make it to the bookshop we would go to our beautifully grand library where we would stagger home with as many books as we were allowed to take out for a week. Just thinking about that shop, and the precious times I spent there with either my mum, dad or brother in my own little world, staring at all the beautiful books on the shelves and remembering where my favourite books were, so that I could rush back the following week to see if they were still there, fills me with the most amazing memories. For me books were magical, precious things, and as a five-, six- and seven-year-old I often wondered how they all got there and who was clever enough to actually write one. I realise now how fortunate I was to have been surrounded by a love of books, to have books of my own from as early as I can remember and to have been encouraged to develop a lifelong love of everything to do with reading. My mum would tell the story of how when I was not much older than a year old I would stand in the middle of our living room, clutching a newspaper, pretending to read it for as long as I could stand. If I had something to read I was happy. It's still the same today.

Library visits, bookshops, jumble sales and pocket money all enabled me to extend my love of all things book related. I would save my pocket money (and any money I was given for my birthday) until I was able to buy a favourite book that I had spent weeks and sometimes months looking at in my favourite shop. Books extended my world, opened up endless possibilities and made my life so much more than it really was. They were my earliest provocations.

Books made me wonder, think, question and experience so many things that were outside of my normality. I couldn't actually go into space or dive into the ocean, or find every beautiful plant and flower I was fascinated with, but I experienced each of these things within the pages of my books. They provoked me in so many ways. For other people, provocations are certainly not books! They are nature, the outdoors, animals, the sea, vehicles, engines, glass beads, buttons, colours or music; the list is endless and as limitless as children's interests and practitioners' imaginations. This is what this book is about, provocations and learning in the early years, and why as a profession we should be taking these things seriously, not only for our children's sake but for their future life chances. I hope you'll be able to either read this in full or dip in and out perhaps when you are looking for some quick provocational ideas or just to check something you have read previously. The Top 10/20 Things and Things to Think About sections are there to help with your reflections and to help with planning.

Now you know a little bit more about me and at least one reason why I wanted to write this book. I also want to try and express why working in this way is important and why it has worked for me. I'm a bit of an 'education geek' and love education books. I think that's why I also love Twitter and all the fantastic education people who contribute their ideas, knowledge and time via Twitter. If you've never had a look I'd really encourage you to be brave and see what's there. I've made some amazing connections and learned so much from joining groups and following education experts, teachers and groups. I also got my book contract as a result of the connections I made on Twitter, so it really has been a life changer for me.

Chapter 1

What Are Provocations and Where Do They Originate?

As an artful educator, you see the world as a place where learning opportunities are scattered everywhere. What might look like a simple roll of sticky tape, a blank envelope or a discarded crisp packet to some people will look like a potential resource for learning to teachers. It is this ability to look at the ordinary and think about using it in an unusual way that shows the power of creative thinking.

Sue Cowley: *The Artful Educator* (2017, p.98)

I have always loved those magical 'Ahhh' moments when one of our youngest learners suddenly sees something, experiences something or makes a new discovery or realisation for the first time. Those are the times we plan for, we reflect upon and we aim to provide a learning and discovery environment for: to enable these amazing young children to discover, experience, learn for the first time, or indeed to re-experience and make sense of something for the first time. Essentially these are the moments we think about, and develop a rich enabling environment for, where every child can explore, investigate, discover and learn. We are privileged because we get to do the thinking, the planning, the organising and the enabling so that we can then share in those eureka discovery moments with the children. We are lucky enough to observe these special moments and build on them for the future.

I was reminded of this very recently when I met a friend and her three-year-old son, Harvey. We used to work together and, as is usually the case, we were discussing school and early years: a mutual love and passion. It was a dull, very humid day and we were sitting outside at a very child-friendly ice-cream parlour and café, which supplies a great range of indoor and outdoor toys for preschool children. As we both possess the 'eyes in the back of your head' thing, we noticed a huge snail shell that was attached to the soft play mat that my friend's son was about to start playing on. As we carefully pointed out the shell to her little boy, the very obliging snail very slowly and deliberately poked its head out of the shell, much to Harvey's delight and curiosity. Fast forward two-and-a-half hours, when we were tidying everything away and the snail was still centre stage, keeping us all interested. Of course what we couldn't have known at the start of the morning was that this beautiful creature would hold out interest and attention for the whole of the time we were there. It had certainly provoked our interest – most importantly that of the youngest member of our group, and he'd loved every second of discovering the snail-trail, why the snail makes it, the way it moved and travelled and the distance it could travel across a range of terrains. The delight and joy it inspired in him made our morning. Obviously, we couldn't have planned for that eventuality, but we could utilise it and make the morning one of discovery and fun. Something as simple as a snail created and supported so much discovery, talk, questioning and learning, and I'm sure the photographs we took will be a lovely reminder of the morning and the discoveries with our lovely Mr Snail.

Personally, it again reminded me of why I love working in this way and how important it is for our youngest children to find themselves in these provocational situations.

Indeed, many things can provoke an unexpected discovery and learning experience. Much can take place in a wide range of environments, and learning experiences can happen even in the simplest of circumstances. Actually, opportunities really are all around us and we just need to be open to them and to be aware of and make use of them as we did during our visit to the garden. I'm so glad I got to experience such a lovely morning with my friend and her fantastic son – three-year-olds really are a never-ending inspiration.

I hope this book will inspire you to work in this way or to give it a much more central place in your work if you already do so. After all, we all love an 'Oh yes' moment; the more we can have in any week, the better.

SO WHAT DOES *PROVOKE* MEAN?

If you asked a hundred different people, say in a *Pointless* quiz question way, you would get a number of different answers, but the *Cambridge English Dictionary* definition of provoke is:

> *Verb* stimulate or give rise to (a reaction or emotion, typically a strong or unwelcome one)

If we look at synonyms this is what we get: arouse, produce, evoke, cause, elicit, induce, inspire, excite, generate.

We then see these meanings: spark off, foster, promote, prompt, trigger, kindle, instigate, precipitate, engender.

The definition then goes on to say:

> Stimulate or incite (someone) to do or feel something, 'a teacher can **provoke** you into working harder'

> Synonyms: goad, spur, prick, sting, prod, egg on, incite, rouse, stir, move, stimulate, motivate, excite, inflame, impel, prompt, induce, encourage, urge, inspire.

It is interesting to compare the synonyms to the words we regularly use within our planning and discussions about the work we plan for and engage in with children. Obviously terms such as goad, prick and sting are not used, but how many times do early years staff use motivate, encourage, stimulate, prompt, inspire, foster, generate, produce, inspire or excite?

If we compare these examples with the vocabulary used in the Early Learning Goals,[1] we see many parallels.

If we look at the most recent inspection framework publications by Ofsted, they state that practitioners should go beyond technical learning:

> The curriculum extends beyond the academic, technical or vocational. It provides for learners' broader developments, enabling them to develop and discover their interests and talents. (Ofsted 2019a, p.11)

To be provoked or to experience provocation can mean different things to different people, and the same can be said when we use this in our settings and with young children. Some people are easily provoked, so they react to things quickly; others are less so and need something more dramatic or personally significant in order for them to be provoked. For example, people with hayfever can be provoked into a reaction simply by being close to certain trees or flowers.

Put simply, provocations provoke. This includes all aspects of learning and development, provoking interest, curiosity, discussion and discovery. They also provoke children's questions, queries, thoughts and ideas.

---

1 See https://www.gov.uk/government/publications/eyfs-profile-exemplication-materials

TOP 20 THINGS THAT PROVOKE LEARNING

- Collections big or small of any type of object
- Collections of things that reflect
- Collections of minibeast toys (soft or plastic)
- Collections of natural objects
- Collections of things with lids with smaller things inside
- Collections of things that make a noise
- Collections of cooking utensils
- Collections of ribbons
- Collections of balls
- Collections of shells
- A box of paper and cards of different colours, sizes and styles
- A large drawstring bag full of numbers: squashy glitter numbers, number tiles, coloured plastic numbers, knitted numbers, numbers made of painted Modroc
- Marbles and paperweights
- Mechanical wind-up toys
- A table set with a tablecloth and 20 different teapots
- An old-fashioned suitcase full of clothes and shoes
- Shoeboxes containing odd shoes: large shoes that are too big for the children
- A large clear beach ball containing glitter
- Something a young child has never seen before: a video player, a Walkman, a portable record player, a butter churn, a flower press, a fountain pen, a bubble pipe
- Ice and resin captures, where small, interesting items such as toys, flowers, glitter, etc. are captured for investigation

Of course, the key to all of these things is that they provoke interest and curiosity in the children, but children also must be given the space and time to play and explore them. It's true that they will not be unusual to adults, but they will be unusual to a young child. Sometimes we get the idea that things are very familiar and that they wouldn't necessarily be of any great interest for a child. In other words, they wouldn't provoke. However, we are looking at this from our adult perspective and what we really need to do is see it through the eyes of a child. We also need to remember that every child has very different previous experiences and so will naturally find different things provocational and of interest. What works for one group of children may have very different results with another, and for me that is one of the joys of provocational learning: neither you nor the children really know where it is going to lead. The possibilities are endless and so are the learning opportunities.

By providing children with collections of objects, and then giving them time to observe, explore and play with them, we enable them to act upon the initial curiosity of the provocational items and develop their understanding through play. Time, space and freedom will enhance the provocation and aid children's play and development in numerous ways, helping them to become more creative, analytical, investigative and critical. As Yogman *et al.* reported through their *Clinical Reports on the Importance of Play* in 2018, 'children who were in active play for one hour per day were better able to think creatively and multitask' (p.6).

When we engage in provocational learning we provide a creative and stimulating environment in which children can fully engage in active play. For some children this will be to simply observe and encounter the collections of objects in this visual way as they build their own understanding. Many others will become engrossed, and develop knowledge and understanding that we may or may not have foreseen. The play will extend their learning and bridge the gap between earlier understanding and newly acquired skills.

ARE PROVOCATIONS NOT JUST ADULT-LED LEARNING?

This question has recently been raised about the use of provocations in the early years. It's always interesting to consider other positions and to dissect other views and standpoints. I can certainly see the reason for the question and also the underlying criticism; after all, adult-led activities demand that the adults plan the overall aim of the session, the objective and create the environment through the resources they plan, select and set up either indoors or outdoors. However, that, I feel, is where the similarities with adult-led learning end.

The adult role in provocations is to recognise the interests of the children, plan and set up a particular provocation and then to observe as the children explore, discover and interact with the resources. Adults can become involved through the use of careful questioning, testing theories or posing ideas, but it is important that the adults do not take over or dominate the play, or indeed have specific outcomes in mind. Provocations are open-ended and should not have pre-planned learning objectives in mind. If the adult(s) do lead the learning in any way, it may be satisfactory for them but it will result in a narrowing both of the learning experience for the child and of the possible range of outcomes that occur naturally when children are provided with full potential to explore.

One major point to remember in all of this is that an adult-led activity can only be adult-led if the adult actually leads. It is true that an adult will have set up the provocation and planned according to the children's interests or, as described later in the book, set a provocation of a more complex type for the children to become engaged in (see Chapters 8, 11 and 19). Provocations are free for the children to explore and there is no obligation for the children to actually engage with them. Adult-led activities are largely guided and directed throughout. Provocations can also simply be a change in resources in a familiar area so that they entice children's interest, gain their attention and then see where things develop. For example, it could be setting out a giant hopscotch mat and a box with giant inflatable numbers. Who knows how the children will respond? Or rearranging the construction area and updating the selection of construction toys that are available for the children to use, adding a slightly more complex selection of items.

Any activity that is often regarded as an indoor activity can also be taught outdoors:

> Anything you can teach in an indoor classroom can be taught outdoors, often in ways that are more enjoyable for children! (Cathy James 2015, p.25)

💡 Things to think about

- Do you know anything about the use of provocations in learning in the early years?

- When was the last time you experienced something similar to my experience with my friend and her son? Does this have any implications for your practice or setting? Do you think of yourself as an 'artful educator' (as described by Sue Cowley)?

- Do you work alongside other professionals who do?

- What is the most 'artful' thing you have done in the past academic year?

Chapter 2

The History, the Theoretical Background and Reggio Emilia

So where does the philosophy of provocations originate from?

Historically, this way of working dates back to Loris Malaguzzi (1920–1994) who was arguably one of the most significant educationalists of the last century. Malaguzzi helped to create a system of public or municipal schools in Reggio Emilia, in northern Italy. It can be argued that it was the most successful example of progressive education that has ever been seen. Some people even regard it as radical. Provocations are one of the cornerstones of Loris Malaguzzi's Reggio Emilia approach and are a significant part of the exploration-based way of discovering and learning:

> What children learn does not follow an automatic result from what is taught, rather, it is in large part due to the children's own doing, as a consequence of their activities and our resources. (Loris Malaguzzi: *The Hundred Languages of Children: The Reggio Emilia Approach to Early Childhood Education*, 1998, p.67)

Reggio Emilia-inspired working requires teachers to use materials and activities, within a framework of a creative environment, to provoke investigations and learning. The intention of the provocation is to focus upon the process of discovery for the children. It is their discovery and their learning that is the most important thing. This way of working can be a new experience for many teachers and educators. As a drama specialist, working with provocations often feels very much like a drama session. In both methods of working the power and responsibility is handed over to the children. The adults do not have 100 per cent control of the learning and, due to the open-ended nature of the work, it can be challenging.

Provocations in early years classrooms and settings have obviously been adapted and evolved, as has almost everything in education to a greater or lesser extent. There are links to Montessori education and its philosophy of exploration and discovery. In recent years Reggio Emilia and Montessori methods have become more prominent in many education systems, particularly in the American system where experts and paediatricians are increasingly focusing on the importance of play in the development of executive functioning skills (Yogman *et al.* 2018). They recognise the strength of these educational philosophies and how they actively support the development of key attributes and competencies that are needed for all children and for their future in the 21st century.

WHY SHOULD WE USE PROVOCATIONS AT THIS TIME?

Personally, I get so excited and motivated about working in this way. I love exploring ideas, connections and resources. Whatever context I see a new thing in, the first thing that comes into my mind is 'How can this be used in school?' I know that I'm not the only person who thinks in this way. When I'm motivated and excited about what I'm doing, the children I'm working with and learning with will also be excited. I recently met an ex-pupil who very sweetly said that she recognised me straight away, despite not having seen me for almost 16 years! She also said I hadn't changed and that she'd loved being in my class because of all the different challenges we did. It made me realise and appreciate that, regardless of what age group I was working with, I had always used provocations in my teaching practice. So why is this method of working important and why do we need to consider it at this point in time?

When I work with teachers and schools throughout the country I often meet early years educators who want to discuss the reasons for working in specific ways. One thing that is always apparent is the passion and dedication that early years educators have and the love they have for working with our youngest children. They passionately want to get it right for them. They are more than aware of the importance of their role supporting children at the start of their school-based education and they want to ensure that the children in their settings get the very best start to their time in school. However, they also realise that early years is a unique stage of a child's education and that so much of their future success depends upon the sensitive handling of these first steps into the wider world of 'school'.

We are certainly in the midst of a period of change in early years, and as educators we cannot ignore or underestimate the impact these changes may have upon our work and the experiences that our youngest children will be exposed to. With changes to the inspection process due to take place from September 2020, the impact of baseline assessments in Reception and implications from an emphasis upon curriculum planning and management, early years staff need to be very secure in the 'why' and 'what' of what they do within their setting and with their planning. Staff need to have security in their personal educational philosophy and how this matches the aims and ethos of their own school. They also need to be aware of the future needs of their children and how their lives will inevitably change within the rapid technological developments that will take place in the next 50 years.

I am convinced that the use of provocations within the early years is a much needed and relevant way of working. I also passionately believe that the key skills that are developed and enhanced through the use of provocations will actively support our children throughout the whole of their future education and also beyond this as they move into the adult world and the world of work.

Every time you turn on the news (or see a newspaper), we are bombarded with information about economics and jobs and what we need to do to be successful. You may wonder what this has to do with early years and what we do in our classrooms. Actually, it has everything to do with what we do. The curriculum we plan and deliver must be appropriate for the skills our children will need in their future and this should be reflected in our school aims and vision statements.

If we consider the children we teach every day, we know what they like, what they enjoy doing and have observed them repeatedly returning to favourite activities time and time again. What we may not have considered is that the future jobs that the majority of our three-year-olds will do have not even been invented or thought of yet! That is a startling thought. It's also a massive implication for our schools, the curriculum we plan and the things that our children engage in. We have an obligation to get this right for our children, and this means that as educators we need to reflect and consider why we do things. It also means that for some people and schools this will need a mindset shift. Can we realistically expect to continue to be pressured into working in more formal ways with our youngest children when we know this is not appropriate or fulfilling for them? Many people would argue that the increased formality of the current curriculum and relentless testing simply does not fit with the future world that our children will work and live in. Sir Ken Robinson argues these very points in his book *Out of Our Minds: The Power of Being Creative* (2017), and his TED Talk *Do Schools*

Kill Creativity? (2006), which is the most watched TED Talk of all time. In both of his works he discusses issues that face all of us, but particularly those of us who are responsible for curriculum design (or 'curriculum intent' – Ofsted 2019a, p.9). Sir Ken provides very powerful arguments for the need to reform and transform the educational experiences that we have traditionally delivered in the past. They, he argues, were derived and needed for children to work in an industrialised nation where they would need skills to enable them to work successfully within this system. Over the last 30 years a shift in power has taken place between traditional jobs such as industrial and manual work to jobs that are based on information technology and providing a service. The rapid development of the gig economy and the practice of remote working have further increased the distance from what many people view as traditional jobs to the ones we see now. Interestingly, he states that dominant global corporations used to be oil and manufacturing but that today they are in the fields of communication, information, entertainment, science and technology. Sir Ken states, 'Our children will not only change jobs several times in their lives but will probably change careers' (Robinson 2017, p.34). He goes on to say:

> We cannot meet the challenges of the twenty-first century with educational ideologies of the nineteenth. We need a new Renaissance that values different modes of intelligence and that cultivates creative relationships between education, commerce and the wider community... The price of failure is more than we can afford and the benefits of success may be more than we imagine. (Robinson 2017, p.237)

If you haven't read Sir Ken's work or watched his talks, they are inspiring and support the provocational method of working as it supports numerous future skills that children will need.

In school we frequently ask ourselves questions such as 'Why are we doing this?' or 'Is this the best way to do this?'; 'What is the aim of this?'; and 'What will the children get from the activity?' In fact as teachers and educators we probably spend a large proportion of our week asking why. I recently spent a whole morning talking about this very thing with a friend (and ex-colleague) when we really weren't supposed to be talking work; we'd actually met for coffee! So if we want to understand why provocations should be an integral part of our work we should really understand who is supporting this way of working and what the reasons for that are.

One organisation that may be a surprising torchbearer of this is the World Economic Forum. While working on this book, I was looking to find support from real-life examples and not just from educational research or historical examples. As I worked my way through various sources I suddenly found some data that seemed to be supporting everything I had been looking for and that also supported the many discussions I'd had with early years professionals across the country. People were looking to justify their practice and were often frustrated and disillusioned by the pervasive drive to introduce increasingly formal methods of working into early years classrooms. We all needed some cold hard data and information from some 'big hitters' that colleagues, senior leaders, governors and outside agencies had to take seriously and couldn't just dismiss as something that was somehow intuitive or 'felt' by an early years professional.

So what exactly did the World Economic Forum have to say and how did it support my needs and those of other professionals?

The World Economic Forum may not naturally seem to be an organisation that would support the work of early years teachers and educators; however, they are an international organisation that supports public and private cooperation. From its base in Geneva, Switzerland, it provides much-needed guidance, information and solutions on world issues including education, innovation, climate change and world working practices.

If you are interested in their work, their Twitter account (@wef) is a really easy way to access their many reports and to see the range of things they are involved with.

I began to realise that my personal views regarding the real demands of an up-to-date curriculum and the numerous discussions I was having with headteachers and education professionals were not just a coincidence. So many people were feeling that we were missing something and that we needed to address the issues now as opposed to somewhere in the future. When I found the World Economic Forum 'The Future of Jobs Report 2018', I knew there was a symmetry between what we wanted and the reality of what economic and industry leaders needed and wanted for now and in the future.

So what did they say?

In 2018, the World Economic Forum issued their findings relating to key skills as identified by employers and industry. They compared these skills to those that will be needed, and most requested by, employers and industry in ten years. When considering the identified skills, what becomes apparent are the stark differences between what are usually regarded as the things that we should be teaching to and developing within our pupils and what they will actually need in their future. As a rule we are still focusing on areas such as formal academic traditional work-related skills and attributes that, as Sir Ken Robinson pointed out, are those needed by an industrialised economy and workplace rather than being based around innovation, creativity, complex problem solving, reasoning, technology design and programming.

At the World Economic Forum Annual Meeting 2019, Stephane Kasriel reported that the next two decades will see a wholesale revolution in our working lives. We know that we are already living in an age of technological revolution, just in the same way that people lived through the Industrial Revolution. Robots, Artificial Intelligence (AI) and the rapidly developing range of everyday tech means that a high percentage of the jobs our three-year-olds will do as adults have not even been invented yet.

Kasriel believes that there are reasons to be hopeful that future jobs will be become more flexible, accessible and even liberating throughout the next two decades and beyond.

These are the five significant changes that have been highlighted for the World Economic Forum:

- AI and robots will create more work as opposed to less.

- There will not be a shortage of jobs, but there may be a shortage of skilled talent to successfully fill those roles if we do not take the right steps now.

- Cities will become the centres for talent wars as we enter a phase where remote working becomes the norm for huge numbers of people.

- By 2027 the majority of the workforce will be freelance (and will have greater geographical freedom to live where they want).

- Technological change will continue, and learning new skills will be an ongoing necessity throughout life.

These things are obviously a challenge to schools and educators, both for our planning and organisation. The World Economic Forum and Kasriel believe that the question we should be asking is, what should we be doing to ensure the most successful and inclusive outcomes?

They make some clear recommendations, as outlined below.

Solution 1: Rethink education

Due to continuous technological changes, people will need to constantly unlearn and learn new skills, and quickly. Educators need to be aware of this and must build an education system for lifelong learning and not just talk about it. School and education cultures must respond rapidly to these changes and build cultures that promote this. The World Economic Forum states that the system should begin with pre-kindergarten, which should be free for all, and compulsory, and that education should remain accessible throughout a person's working life to respond to the technological challenges.

Solution 2: A plan for the future

From all of this we can see that there is and will be a need to plan for the development and specific teaching and learning of key skills that will enable the future workforce to be successful, adaptable lifelong learners with a strong sense of creativity and flexibility.

Many influential people, including industry and world leaders, such as Michelle Obama, the Clinton Institute, the RSA, the LEGO® group and IKEA, are supporting such developments. As previously noted, Sir Ken Robinson is one of the most outspoken and convincing advocates of the need for creativity in education. In his book *Out of Our Minds: The Power of Being Creative* (2017), Robinson puts forward the case for creating environments that build creativity and the need to do this now. He delivers hard-hitting reasons as to why schools and educators have to lead this change in response to the technological challenges we face, and that the key to this is to create the much-needed creative environments.

> Teaching for creativity involves asking open ended questions where there may be multiple solutions; working in groups on collaborative projects, using imagination to explore possibilities; making connections between different ways of seeing and exploring the ambiguities and tensions that may lie between them. (Robinson 2017, p.227)

It is not just Sir Ken Robinson who is on a mission to change the way countries teach their children. The head of the education division of the Organisation for Economic Co-operation and Development (OECD), Andreas Schleicher, feels that society is preparing children for the world of work in totally the wrong way. At the Learn It Conference in London in January 2019 he said:

> We are scared that human jobs will be replaced by robots. But we are still teaching kids to think like machines.

He went on to argue that creativity, questioning and collaboration are the key skills that we should be teaching our children:

> What we know is that the kind of things that are easy to teach, and maybe easy to test, are precisely the kind of things that are easy to digitise and to automate.

During his presentation he also said that it is easy to teach and test for maths but that robots are good at maths too. The skills that Schleicher wants world educators to emphasise are those things that robots and computers cannot do alone: human skills of collaboration, working together, imagining, creating and questioning.

Jack Ma, the former head of the Chinese e-commerce giant Alibaba, supported the views of Sir Ken Robinson and Andreas Schleicher when he spoke at the World Economic Forum in 2018. Ma argued that unless educators focus upon redesigning the curriculum and teaching the skills that are uniquely human – independent thinking, teamwork, caring for others – children simply don't stand a chance:

> If we do not change the way we teach our children in 30 years we will be in big trouble.

Schleicher and Ma both believe that the industrial model of education needs to change. Ma believes that the solution is to change from a model where students are shuttled through an assembly line of subjects and tests to a system where formal testing is a much more measured approach. Indeed, Schleicher, who oversees the Programme for International Student Assessment (PISA) tests, has been waging a revolution to change the focus of the PISA tests from Maths, Science and Reading to a test that measures those things that are needed for future success in the technologically rich 21st century – empathy, creativity, competencies, mindsets and skills. New additional tests that PISA have introduced include those focusing upon problem solving and global competencies. In 2021 it will begin to include creative thinking and being inquisitive and persistent.

If this is the future for PISA, and it continues to play a major part in the comparative assessment of education systems, our schools at every level must respond and do so quickly. With influential educators and thinkers advocating major changes in the fundamental structure and content of our education systems not only for the benefit of our children, but for industries and commerce too, we cannot stand to one side and wait while other countries change and grow. With flexible working patterns, remote and distance working and global connectivity, children in our country will be competing with people from across Europe and the world for future jobs and personal security. If we genuinely care about our children and their future, we have got to be decisive, brave and forward thinking in meeting these very real technological challenges and rapidly build the exciting and appropriate curriculum and school system that they will need.

Despite many teachers and educators' issues with Ofsted and the recent inspection system within England, it can be argued that the revised education inspection framework (Ofsted 2019a), which came into effect from September 2019, is making definite strides to meet the challenges voiced by people like Sir Ken Robinson, Jack Ma and Andreas Schleicher of the OECD. A major criticism of the inspection process and the influence of Ofsted has been that it has been directly responsible for the narrowing of the curriculum and the pervasive assessment and test regime that has taken hold of so many aspects of our schools. Add to this the ever-present and growing issues with young people's mental health and wellbeing and the connections that are made between the relentless testing systems throughout schools and these serious issues and it isn't hard to see that changes need to be made. It can be argued that HM Chief Inspector Amanda Spielman has indeed responded to these complicated and multi-layered issues with the revised Framework and Handbooks and the emphasis upon curriculum and the changes that need to take place.

The emphasis really is firmly based upon the curriculum and what schools and settings will be offering to their children. Headteachers are being told to be bold in their curriculum design to provide the very best for the children in their schools. This is a perfect time to review the curriculum on offer and determine what really is unique about what you offer your pupils, making clear links to the school's ethos and values. In a time when we are being told to be brave, be brave. Build and develop the curriculum that the children will need for their future and provide them with a rich, enabling environment that builds 21st century skills. The links to the use of provocations is obvious.

In May 2019, Ofsted published the outcomes from its consultation on the new education inspection framework that came into effect from September 2019. From this information, it is clear that there has been a shift, and a major one at that. Indeed this consultation is the largest Ofsted has ever undertaken – the result of almost two years' research and engagement with teachers, headteachers and other stakeholders – since its instigation over 20 years ago.

HM Chief Inspector Amanda Spielman said:

The new framework puts real substance of education at the heart of inspection and supports leaders and teachers who act with integrity. We hope early years, schools and college leaders will no longer feel the need to generate and analyse masses of internal data for inspection. Instead, we want them to spend time teaching and making a real difference to children's lives, which is why they entered the profession in the first place. (cited in Ofsted 2019b)

In the new framework, curriculum really is king, and of course this will influence and affect what nurseries and early years settings do in response to the changes. The question that I am often asked and that is frequently discussed is: why should the inspection process influence what we plan and do? My response from this point in time is: why not? If we are to believe the new documentation and to become actively engaged in this process in a positive and strategic way, then this is a huge opportunity for setting and staff to build a curriculum they actually believe in passionately and to use this to open up and engage in a real dialogue with Ofsted that illustrates what their setting does that is unique and special for their children and learners.

Ofsted use the term 'refocus' in the inspection process to:

make sure that learners are receiving a high-quality education that puts them on a path to future success (Ofsted 2019c)

and also state that:

inspectors will spend less time looking at exam results and test data, and more time considering how a nursery, school…has achieved their results. That is, whether they are the outcome of a broad, rich curriculum and real learning, or of teaching to the test…to focus on what children actually learn, ahead of results… (Ofsted 2019c)

Most recently, discussions about education have been dominated by talk of curriculum intent. Everyone certainly has a view on this and it has generated some interesting thoughts and projections regarding what exactly is meant by this phrase. In the early years there are obviously certain pedagogical views, as we must consider the developmental stages that the children are at when we plan and organise our curriculum. One of the major differences between the way we refer to our children and other age groups is that we use months. This is both to show how young these children really are and to remind ourselves that their development changes across and through these age ranges from birth to 60 months.

According to Heather Fearn, in *Busting the Intent Myth* via Gov.uk July 2019:

> But at its heart, intent is about the substance of education: What do you want pupils to know? ...we're talking about how ambitious, coherently planned and sequenced, how broad and balanced and inclusive the curriculum is.

She goes on to say intent really is a simple concept and is about what school leaders actually want, i.e. what they intend the pupils to learn. She says it is everything that happens, up to the point at which teaching happens, and that good intent has the following features:

- A curriculum that is:

  - ambitious for all pupils

  - coherently planned and sequenced

  - successfully adapted, designed and developed for pupils with special educational needs and/or disabilities

  - and is broad and balanced for all pupils.

(Adapted from Fearn 2019)

This is a perfect opportunity to reflect upon what our curriculum statements do include. Many representatives from Ofsted have gone on record to say that there is no need to attend a course or pay additional money to produce curriculum intent statements. We should have the courage of our convictions and look to what we believe; as early years practitioners, we know that our intent will be, and should be, different from other key stages of education. Our intent is to actively develop young children's key dispositions, attitudes and skills. We know that we will be doing this through play and that we will be planning our continuous development to do so. This is where our intent statements and accompanying documentation need to be clear about why play is such an important part of our work and how it enables our youngest children to learn and develop.

A recently published research paper by Michael Yogman and colleagues called 'The power of play: a pediatric role enhancing development in young children' (Yogman *et al.* 2018) not only supports the need for play and its importance in the development of young children but states that children need to develop a number of skill sets in order to optimise their development and manage toxic stress, and that play is key to this. They state in their abstract that research demonstrates that play that is developmentally appropriate is an opportunity to promote:

> the social-emotional, cognitive, language and self-regulation skills that build executive function and a prosocial brain… play is not frivolous: it enhances brain structure and function and promotes executive function (i.e. the process of learning, rather than context), which allows us to pursue goals and ignore distractions. (Yogman *et al.* 2018, p.1)

They go on to state that play is fundamental for the learning and development of 21st century skills such as problem solving, collaboration and creativity, which require the executive functioning skills that are critical for adult success. They also highlight the commitment of the United Nations Convention on the Rights of the Child which has enshrined the right of the child to engage in play that is appropriate to the age of the child (Article 21). This applies to all children, of all ages, all over the world. We would do well to remember this when we are planning for our enabling environments and when we are involved in professional discussions about why Early Childhood Education (ECE) is so important and why we value play so highly.

Here again is a similar view to those of Sir Ken Robinson and the World Economic Forum regarding future work skills and the development work of Andreas Schleicher and Jack Ma. This actively supports the argument for play and for provocational play – our children need it for their future success and for their health and wellbeing. Interestingly, the most recently released figures from the Department for Digital, Culture, Media & Sport revealed that the creative industries have grown at nearly twice the rate of the economy since 2010. In 2018, the UK's creative industries broke through the £100 billion mark, making a record contribution to the UK economy (Department for Digital, Culture, Media & Sport and the Rt Hon Jeremy Wright 2018). Film, TV, radio, photography, music, advertising, galleries and digital creative industries are all part of this rapidly thriving sector. This is also the case with the digital and tech industries that are world leaders. Schools and the education sector in general must therefore recognise the growing importance of the creative and digital sectors and support and prepare our children effectively with the skills they will need in the future. We need to be supporting these things now. The use of provocational learning provides us with a framework to do this.

⬦ Things to think about

- How much do you already know about Reggio Emilia?

- Have you ever visited a setting where they use this?

- How often do you use provocations in your work?

- Do you think there is a place for provocations in your practice?

- What are your reactions to the information from the World Economic Forum?

- Do you think that education should be more closely tailored to the skills children will need in the future?

- Has anything that you have read made you want to find out more?

- Is there anyone you would like to share this information with and discuss it further?

- What are the implications for you as a teacher and educator?

- Will any of this change your future practice?

Chapter 3

The Ethos of Using Provocations

When I work with teachers and schools I often find myself involved in discussions regarding ethos and school aims and how these match to the early years. We have all spent time working on school statements of some kind and/or producing information for parents and carers that aims to show why our setting is unique, special and a place where children will thrive. Very often we produce vision or mission statements that, if we are honest, sound rather similar to those of other schools and in reality don't capture the real nature of our school and the things that are important to us. If that comes across as a criticism, it isn't meant to be – I am just trying to be honest about a common problem. The problem is that we are all trying to capture the unique essence of what we believe in, and that is difficult. Add to that the number of different views that a large number of staff will have regarding educational aims and it turns into a complex situation. I actually think that what early years staff need to do is to consider what they actually do that promotes those key values. What specific methods do they use that demonstrate their key values, aims and objectives? Are there certain systems in place that do this or ways of teaching and learning that support these aims? In other words, what do they do that actively shows their ethos?

You only have to get a number of early years staff into a room together to know that there are a number of 'umbrella things' that the majority of people and settings do. These are the core aspects of the curriculum and of what practitioners do. However, once we move past these things, we begin to see the very specific elements that make individual settings, and therefore individual children's experiences, special.

If you consider the local schools and settings you are each familiar with, you probably know of some that are passionate about Forest Schools or outdoor learning, others that have huge passions about the arts and arts education, and others with STEM (science, technology, engineering and mathematics) at the heart of their learning. Some schools build their ethos around spiritual, moral, social and cultural education and others around academic excellence. These are the things that get communicated to our parents and the wider community, but my question is, how often do we include key elements of early years learning such as cooperating, collaborating, questioning, working together and discovering in our key messages? Surely key skills and attributes are what we should be including, and if we are, then perhaps we could make this even more specific and go on to include ways of learning. This is where I see provocations being included, and this is why. When we talk about our aims and ethos as I have already mentioned, what we frequently refer to is overarching things, the things that parents and the wider community are more familiar with. At this point in time, where we have a newly revised inspection framework and an emphasis upon moving forward in our drive to develop an outstanding curriculum, I feel we should be including information regarding our use of provocations and how they actively support vital elements of our vision statements and school ethos. After all, if these statements include things like wanting to have lifelong, independent learners, or children that collaborate and can solve problems, provocations and their use as a specific method of learning can do this for us. The ethos of provocations takes us back to the original work of Loris Malaguzzi and his pioneering work in

Reggio Emilia (see Chapter 2), where children were engaged in a unique learning environment. These children became lifelong learners through being immersed in the unique environment that encouraged and developed the key skills and attributes that they would need in the future.

TOP 10 THINGS FOR A QUICK PROVOCATION

- Move your furniture around
- Rearrange your reading/story area
- Add some light to something
- Tent an area and leave a selection of torches
- Put a collection of fluffy/sparkly/different pens in your writing area
- Use some small world resources from another class
- Add some oversized soft toys to an area
- Soften an area by adding soft materials
- Paint something
- Put up some wallpaper in the role-play area

Chapter 4

The Power of Play

We are all familiar with Maria Montessori's idea that play is the child's work (1967). If you google quotes about play you can spend hours immersed in a world of amazing people who recognise just how and why play is such an important part in the development of a child and why we must plan and organise our rooms and settings to fully support young children's play.

Personally, I believe that children should be able to play for far longer than we currently allow them to do in this country. We are always being told by numerous education ministers that we should look to Scandinavian countries. I totally agree, and that means play being at the heart of our work and that all children should be playing for longer. Some of the best schools and classrooms I have visited have been those where play is planned for and encouraged right up to Year 6. Alleluia to that!

In 2008, Vivian Gussin Paley delivered a keynote speech to the Wonderplay Early Childhood Learning Conference where she, as always, delivered a powerful message about the critical importance of play, particularly imaginative play. She has always been an inspiration for me as an early years teacher and leader, and revisiting this has reminded me why we need to develop and spread a powerful argument about why we create play-based enabling environments in our settings.

In her keynote speech Gussin Paley discusses how every species of young mammal engages in play and practises being young; they do this through jumping, running, pushing, climbing, bumping, pulling and pouncing, and these are necessary survival skills. When discussing human children she goes on to say that they must add another survival skill, that imaginative play of pretending to be another person in another time and place, making up character, plot and dialogue for the stories they invent as they play:

> They are in truth inventing abstract thinking, the act of stepping outside one-self and viewing a broader perspective of relationships, verbal, visual, social, physical. But they are also, it seems to me, inventing reading, writing and arithmetic, all in an earlier primitive form in preparation for... They are inventing and reinventing themselves as thinking people before the world tells them what to think. (Gussin Paley 2008)

You only have to have spent time observing young children in their imaginative play to completely understand what she means by inventing reading, writing and arithmetic in an earlier primitive form. Children coming up to you and showing their writing, making shapes, numbers and patterns in loose parts play, exploring in the outdoors and garden areas reading signs on gates, plants and trees – our youngest children are always inventing and reinventing, and we need to build effective enabling learning environments that help them to keep doing this. And this is why play is so important. Gussin Paley continues by exploring the child's motivation in their creative play, talking of their own self-knowledge and quiet confidence in their ability and what they are doing. She sees children as inventors who own their play and use it to grow and develop and, ultimately, survive.

> The child says I am someone with ideas. I am someone who turns ideas into actions and actions into new ideas... I am intended to have my own ideas, that's why I play the way I do, to show myself, what my ideas are and how necessary I am to my community. (Gussin Paley 2008)

We must be the people who support our children in this valuable job, in their 'work', as they develop their ideas through creative play, inventing and reinventing, adapting and refining as they move through childhood.

An assessment and testing system that emphasises formal test results (from the start of a child's time in school until they leave), rushes children from a play and discovery-based experience to formal, abstract learning far too quickly. Throughout the country, schools are spending hundreds of thousands of pounds per year on additional support and intensive catch-up programmes where children with learning gaps are taken away from the enabling environments they need to spend time in and placed in small withdrawal groups where they focus, in formal ways, upon the things they should be discovering and developing their understanding of through play. Infant schools cancel afternoon 'play times' because they need to focus on catch-up programmes and wonder why the young, summer-born boys are not achieving the formal results they want to see in the Year 1 phonics screening check. There are students in secondary schools who struggle to understand fractions and fundamental mathematical skills. I attribute all of this to the fact that they missed out on play. They were rushed from concrete stages to formal abstract ones far too soon, expected to sit still, take part in pencil and paper-based activities and deprived of regular outdoor play, fresh air and exercise that would have actively supported their much-needed development. If we work in the early years we must champion play and the development that takes place because of it and not be scared to do so. We may need to support our argument and play-based perspectives with evidence- and power-based positions. They are out there, and becoming ever more visible and influential. Organisations such as More Than a Score and Early Excellence, teachers' unions – including the Association of School and College Leaders and National Education Union – and local authority councils support this view. More surprising perhaps is that support also comes from international organisations which fully recognise why play is so important to children and for their future life chances, including their future roles within the community and in the economy.

The Real Play Coalition was formed in 2018 by the LEGO® Foundation, IKEA, National Geographic and Unilever as they came together with a powerful shared vision regarding children's play:

> to promote play-based opportunities that develop a breadth of skills for optimal child development. (p.12)

THE REAL PLAY COALITION, WORLD ECONOMIC FORUM GENERAL MEETING 2018

The World Economic Forum and the Real Play Coalition know that there is a 'play-gap' and they know that play is the rocket fuel of child development. They are determined to close that gap and reverse the trend in the decline in time children of all ages spend playing, in the number of community play spaces and in the range of opportunities that children from all communities are given. They have carried out a global play study, the *Value of Play Report*, to analyse the range and quality of play and to identify the play-gaps (Real Play Coalition 2018). They know that, throughout the world, children are spending less time playing in favour of traditional academic learning, which is starting earlier and earlier. With schools increasingly focusing on testing and examination and offering less playful experiences, and preschools including greater didactic components than they did 20 years ago, the study found that children were declaring at a rate of one in five that they are 'too busy to play'.

The fourth Industrial Revolution, or the technical revolution as it is sometimes referred to, is about two key things, both interlinked and part of the world that the children we teach will live in: 1) the changes to technology and business and the move to solve global issues including climate change, and 2) the way our children grow up. The Real Play Coalition recognises that we must act now and equip every child with the skills they will need to embrace the technological realities of the 21st century. Their answer is to allow children to develop through play. Some of their early findings are as follows:

- We need to do this if we are to address the looming skills crisis that low-play and play-poverty is creating.

- In the UK, outdoor play has declined by 50% in a generation.

- One in 10 children do not get any outdoor play.

- Children from disadvantaged backgrounds are 20% less likely to play with blocks.

- And 11% less likely to sing songs with their parents.

- Children from high socio-economic families are 10% more likely to engage in all types of play recorded.

- Five-year-old boys are more likely to engage in block play than five-year-old girls.

- Construction block play is related directly to the development of language, motor and early mathematical skills.

- 92% of children say they want more play in their lives.

- 93% of children say play makes them feel happier.

- 83% of children say they learn better when it feels like play.

- Researchers in South Africa found that children who play at home are one-third more likely to have higher executive functioning skills.

- Research carried out by the UK Government found play-based learning improves the academic and emotional development of early years children.

- A German study of Kindergartens reported children who learned through play were more advanced in reading, maths and social skills and also more creative (study across 37 countries RPC 2019).

(Adapted from Miller and Almon 2009)

Right now, according to the Real Play Coalition, our children need to be strengthening the skills they need for the future, those skills that will help them to work productively with technology including creativity, collaboration and communication.

If you are interested in finding out more from Davos and from the Real Play Coalition, including their report, search www.realplaycoalition.com and the following hashtags will lead to many different articles including links to key industry and business leaders' views and direct intentions: #DirtisGood; #RealPlayCoalition; and #futureleaders.

Another excellent source of information regarding play research conducted by Cambridge University is PEDAL: the Centre for Research on Play in Education, Development and Learning,[1] and The Yidan Prize,[2] which is the world's largest education prize.

---

1   https://www.educ.cam.ac.uk/centres/pedal
2   https://yidanprize.org

TOP 10 THINGS TO CREATE PROVOCATIONS OUTSIDE

- Use treasure baskets or boxes or bags
- Use hide and seek activities
- Use something really large!
- Bury things
- Plant things – for children to 'discover' during outdoor play
- Plant flowers, fruit, vegetables or anything that grows
- Use water
- Freeze things in balloons and let them thaw
- Add costumes
- Make it loud! Music, songs, wind chimes, instruments, drums, anything

---

The importance of high-quality, well-resourced outdoor play for the development of children's positive mental health and wellbeing cannot be overestimated. Ensuring it happens is a huge challenge for everyone. With children of all ages reporting concerns about their mental health (Children's Commissioner 2019), our challenge is how to tackle this problem and provide children with the play they need to support their health and wellbeing. According to the Open University's OPENspace Research Centre there is considerable evidence to support outdoor play and experiences (Ward Thompson, Aspinal and Montarzino 2008). They have found that spending time in nature increases a child's ability to concentrate and function in school, improves wellbeing, reduces symptoms of stress and depression and increases life expectancy. Recent data suggests that the positive benefits of being and learning in the outdoors can last up to seven hours after spending 30 to 40 minutes outside (Pritchard 2018). The importance of providing outdoor play and experiences for children is emphasised by the Real Play Coalition, who believe in the power of play and its direct links to happiness, health and discovery:

> The coalition members have a responsibility to help tackle the issues and reclaim play as a path to happiness, connection, escape, learning, self-expression and discovery throughout life. (Real Play Coalition 2018, p.12)

TOP 10 THINGS TO PROVOKE PLAY

- Use a collection of multi-coloured transparent loose parts
- Use a box with a key (full of a mystery collection)
- Use ice balloons
- Use the 'wrong colours' for something!
- Add a scent or use a natural oil
- Add something electronic
- Wrap something up and make a parcel
- Put two unlinked resources together (be brave)
- Add mirrors
- Ooh, and *always* dinosaurs!

 Things to think about

- Would you be the teacher or educator you are today without your own childhood play? Do your parents and carers understand why play is used within your setting?

- What methods do you use that practically involve parents and carers in play within your classroom and in the outdoors?

- Are there any ways in which you could extend play at home through the involvement of your home–school links?

- Could play practices be enriched by regularly involving older Key Stage 1 and Key Stage 2 children throughout the term and the year?

- Do you have evidence of the positive effects of being outdoors on children's mental health and wellbeing?

Chapter 5

Setting Up Your Classroom and Outdoor Learning for Provocations

Because children aren't data, obedience isn't engagement, silence isn't respect, teaching isn't memorising and there is always another way.

Vic Goddard, Principal (2018)

Autonomy, independence, concentration, motivation, observation, challenge, risk, concepts, knowledge – understanding all of these things can be regarded as part of the early years curriculum. When planning, setting up and revising our indoor and outdoor environment throughout the year, I regularly go back to a quote by Fisher, which always reminds me of the Dylan Thomas poem *Do Not Go Gentle Into That Good Night*. They both refer to a rage, or power, of knowing and responding – Fisher to the child's natural curiosity and their need to know, and Thomas to the older person in the twilight of their life and their passion to not simply give in to old age:

> We need to feed the child's natural curiosity, the urge to explore, to try things out, to look more closely, to see what happens. We need to build on a child's disposition to explore and investigate, to satisfy the *rage to know*. (Fisher 1990, p.52)

If we want children to follow their natural curiosity and their urges to explore, to observe closely, to try and make discoveries, we need to provide a comprehensive and stimulating environment in which this can happen. This is our ongoing challenge; it is not simply enough to just reproduce what has gone before in earlier years and to replicate the environments that have been successful for previous cohorts of children. We need to be aware of the holistic nature of the children's learning and also of their needs. We must first observe and study the children to understand their needs and we need to develop effective and trusting relationships with children so that they are confident and happy enough to share their passions and their likes and dislikes with us and know that we will respond and support them in their learning and be their champions. As Rita F. Pierson, the American teacher and educator, said in her acclaimed TED Talk:

> every child deserves a champion: an adult who will never give up on them, who understands the power of connection and insists they become the best they can possibly be. (2013)

If you haven't heard Pierson's talk, I would urge you to find the time to watch it. If you are ever having a bad day, I guarantee that watching it again will lift and inspire you.

Being able to ignite and develop a child's passion, their 'rage to know', and establishing yourself as a champion of the children in your class, may seem a daunting task. But in reality we have all done this already in so many ways. By being a reflective practitioner and through re-evaluating the learning environment you plan and create each week, term and year, you are instinctively doing this. By reflecting upon how your internal and external environments can be improved and refined, you are committing yourself to igniting their 'rage to know' and acting as their champion; for who else can build the appropriate world in which they explore, investigate, take risks, challenge and build their learning?

We all inherit our learning spaces from someone. That is unless we are in the very fortunate position to find ourselves in a new-build school where we genuinely are starting from scratch. The closest I have come to 'starting from scratch' is in the mid-1990s when I was responsible for early years and Key Stage 1 at a very large primary school and I was tasked with establishing a new nursery unit. I had to plan everything – it really was a blank slate – and it was so much harder than I initially anticipated. We take so much for granted when we enter a classroom and we expect that we will have all the basics we need to cover the curriculum and to enable us to deliver the things we have planned. When considering the intricacies of the early years classroom, both inside and outside, we need to recognise that it is a complicated place. Whatever we do to plan for this, we need constantly to remind ourselves that we are not planning for ourselves, or for other adults, but for the children who come through the doors every morning. I think this quote from the DfES from 2007 hits the nail on the head:

> it is important to remember that no plan written weeks in advance can include a group's interest in a spider's web on a frosty morning or a particular child's interest in transporting small objects in a favourite blue bucket, yet it is these interests which may lead to some powerful learning.

THE EARLY YEARS FOUNDATION STAGE: STATUTORY FRAMEWORK FOR THE EARLY YEARS FOUNDATION STAGE AND GUIDANCE FOR THE EARLY YEARS FOUNDATION STAGE (DFES 2007A)

Despite dating back to 2007, this framework will always be relevant to ECE and to anyone who teaches in the early years. Our challenge is to be able to keep this as an ongoing prompt and use this as a benchmark when we are planning our internal and external environment. It is particularly so when we are considering planning for the use of provocations and the role they play in our continuous provision.

A good way to start the planning process is to ask ourselves a few questions regarding our internal and outdoor environment. These questions are linked to the overall planning and development process, but also to the use of provocations. Here are some of the questions that I ask when I am working at this stage:

- Have we considered the indoor and outdoor spaces as separate entities?

- Do we have an accurate, up-to-date audit of the resources we have and their quality?

- Have we discarded all broken, damaged or unsuitable resources?

- Have we highlighted a programme of repair for things that can be repaired (particularly useful for larger equipment and outdoor fixed items, that must be assessed each half term)?

- Do any longer-term developments need to take place ready for the start of a new school year?

- What are my budget limits and do I have to remain within curriculum aspect funding outlines?

- Are there any additional or external funding streams that I can access?

- Is there a possibility to ask for support and provision of resources via parents/local community/other groups?

- Can we access any specialist resource boxes/packs from local education charities or specialists?

- Have we planned for a learning space that is inviting to children? (Think height, shape, structure, space.)

- Have we planned and set up this appropriately? Are there any safety issues?

- Have we created an interesting and intriguing space both internally and externally for each specific aspect of learning?

- Can children investigate?

- Can children observe?

- Can children find quiet, reflective areas that enable them to learn through observation and non-active play?

- Are the resources readily accessible for all children?

- Are there things in place to support challenge, risk and adventurous play, and investigation across the inside and outside learning environment?

- Are we providing gender-specific or gender-biased activities?

- Have we planned and provided areas where children can leave precious ongoing projects that they can return to at a later time?

- Have we communicated our aims to other staff/parents and carers/school leaders/governors and other groups?

🔆 Things to think about

- All of the above prompts and questions.

- Consider how you communicate your educational philosophy and reasons for doing things to your stakeholders, internally and externally, starting with parents and carers, the senior leadership team and the headteacher, who may not be an early years specialist.

- How do you share your practice with other members of your school team? Do they have a clear understanding about the provision you provide, the enabling environments you create and the reasons behind this?

- *The indoor and outdoor environment*: How easily do these areas lend themselves to using provocations? Do you need to add anything or make any small or long-term changes in order to accommodate your planning or to enable the children to become fully engaged in their discoveries and explorations?

- *Display environment*: Are you using your display environment to fully support your use of provocations? Are they helping to inform your parents and carers of what is happening within your setting and how your children are working?

- *Resources and storage*: Provocations and using them to their full potential is a resource implication. A range of resources are detailed in other areas of the book and will help you to consider things that you may want to use. You certainly need to adapt your large and small-scale resources to accommodate the objects, collections and artefacts that you will be using. Open storage areas and cabinets make a brilliant base for storing easily accessible small parts and other resources. Collections of boxes, bags, cases and storage cubes all help to make provocations shine.

- *Books*: Books are a constant inspiration for provocations and for adding another dimension to the provocations that you use, bringing additional information to the children and helping them to develop their explorations and investigations. The illustrations in a book can be just as powerful in sparking a provocation as a text or a whole story. Book displays, cabinets, themed book tables and book walls are all parts of provocations and their use within early years areas. A list of books that can support provocations can be found in the Further Resources section.

Chapter 6

What Things Provoke Young Children?

The quickest answer to this is anything and everything.

The longer answer is things that interest your children. These interests may be brief or longer-lasting, but they will and do change throughout the time the children are with you. Just as the children grow and develop, so do the things that interest them and thus provoke them into action and discovery. The role of the teacher and facilitator is to be fully aware of this and respond accordingly. Children are interested in topical things, and these can apparently come out of nowhere. It may be a school-wide craze for finger spinners or trading cards for the Women's World Cup, or it may be something local and very specific to your setting and school. Keep your ears and eyes open – if you capture this energy, the learning can be tremendous.

On a personal level, this is why I have always listened to the same music that the children are listening to, made the effort to watch the films they are going to see and paid attention to what suddenly arrives on the side of lunch boxes, bags and pencil cases. These can be the things that make a provocation and help children to feel really connected to their learning, and we all know how powerful that is, both as a teacher and a learner.

Here is a list of the things that provoke children and their interests. It is by no means comprehensive but it does cover a large number of aspects; I'm sure you can think of others too.

- Funny things

- Unusual things

- Mysterious items

- Historical artefacts

- Things from different places – the park, the beach, a farm, an office, a dentist surgery, a garage, etc.

- Items from other countries

- Things from different continents

- Items that reflect different cultures

- Religious artefacts

- Uniforms

- Collections of things – shoes and boots, gloves, hats, buttons, bottles, containers, natural items, man-made things, collections of unique materials

- Books – 3D, lift-the-flap, zig-zag, soft books and board books, picture books that cater to all ages and not just Reception class (YR), fact and fiction, old and new, favourite stories in a different language, maps, atlases, road maps, comics and graphic novels, manga

- Book collections and displays

- Mark-making materials

- Shiny objects

- Things that you can see through

- Reflective objects

- Metal items (including rusty items)

- Opaque things

- Collections with a chronology – cameras, mobile phones, keys, shoes or trainers, passports

- Boxes

- Cases and old suitcases or trunks

- Sets of items that are all the same colour – these can be themed, such as different-sized red buttons, or random, such as blue things

- Tactile things, including different textures – smooth, soft, silky, rough, jagged, fluffy

- Unusual shoes

- Reading glasses and sunglasses, including novelty ones

- Handbags and bags in general

- Superhero costumes

- Puppets of all kinds

- Hats

- Things that make noises

- Favourite characters from books, TV, film, etc.

- Cartoon characters

- Unusual objects in their own right

If we take one of the above things, let's explore what could be included in a collection:

FUNNY THINGS

Four-year-olds adore funny things. If you've ever experienced sharing a classroom with children of this age, you'll know exactly what I mean; and they often find things that aren't actually funny hysterical! And that in itself is funny. Knowing what makes children laugh or having something at your fingertips that can break an unhappy or sad moment can be an absolute lifesaver for that individual child and can make a world of difference to them. I remember so many occasions when something quite unexpected has resulted in a mass giggling session and suddenly the whole mood in a room is changed for the better. I honestly think one of the best sounds you can ever hear in a school is children laughing. There should be more of it.

Songs and rhymes are a never-ending source of amusement for young children – the funnier and more complicated, the better. Tongue twisters, list songs, nonsense rhymes, counting songs with funny endings, traditional songs and of course poems, especially by Michael Rosen, are all part of the repertoire.

I've made a point of collecting things that can amuse all my classes and that they find funny. They can often be integrated into other areas of the curriculum and used in numerous situations, so they are never wasted. The children love returning to them and they can form the basis of many provocations; particularly when you need something quickly to put a smile on the face of an unhappy, worried or sad child.

So here are some ideas that can be included in your 'Funny box':

- Anything that makes a noise or squeak (especially a whoopee cushion)
- Things that wobble: jelly, slime, goo, stretchy cobwebs
- Things that surprise them, e.g. an old-fashioned Jack-in-a-Box

- Unusual or unexpected headwear: teachers and adults wearing hats inside, shower caps, sports caps, jesters hats
- Anything oversized (use in role-play areas)
- Wind-up toys, especially if they fall over or something falls off!
- Puppets: sock-puppets, hand puppets, singing puppets, finger puppets
- Emoji cushions (especially the smiley and poo cushion)
- Masks (including famous face masks of people they recognise)
- Bouncy eggs!
- Rubber chickens
- Rubber hairdressers gloves filled with coloured water and placed in water play
- Play snow
- Coloured spaghetti and pasta
- Monster/ghost/scary toys
- Wobbly pens, pencils and pens with tops, glitter, feathers, bobbles, etc.
- Squashy play fruit (available from Tiger)
- Balloons, especially if they have confetti, etc. inside them
- Inflatable toys
- Glitter footballs

One of the funniest resources I have ever used is a singing goat hand puppet that I bought from The Book People over 15 years ago. It is quirky to look at, has off-centre eyes and immediately makes children giggle! Once it starts to sing, things really get silly as it sings 'The Lonely Goatherd' from *The Sound of Music*. The possibilities of making children laugh are endless.

What strikes me as I look at the list is that it could contain so many more things and that almost anything can, and often does, interest and provoke the interest of individual children. As educators and early years practitioners, we need to be constantly aware of that. The challenge is how we react to that and build it into our regular practice so that we effectively support individual interests in the classroom and outdoors.

I am also reminded of the Victorian practice of Cabinets of Curiosity, or *Wunderkammern* (meaning a cabinet of wonder or a wonder room), based on the Italian Renaissance collections that were housed in cabinets of curiosities. The Victorians originally designed and used whole rooms to display the things they had collected on their travels throughout Europe and their grand tours. The use of Cabinets of Curiosity meant that they could keep permanent displays of their most treasured items and share these with other people when they returned to England. It also takes me back to the stunning V&A Alexander McQueen *Savage Beauty* retrospective that took place in 2015 which included an indescribable Cabinet of Curiosity room where original design pieces were displayed alongside work by co-collaborators Shaun Leane and Philip Treacy, along with items and objects that they had been inspired by. It really was a treasure trove and felt like stepping into the inside of a collector's mind. If you work with young children this concept will not be unfamiliar to you, as so many young children have a passion for collecting, storing and keeping small items. A wonderful way of building upon the idea of keeping collections to inspire and provoke learning and to enable children to share their passions is to make and use a Cabinet of Curiosity. I would even suggest having a permanent cabinet in the outdoors and one inside the classroom. They can be used in two main ways. First, to enable children to display their items generically or within a particular theme, and second, as a means to stimulate interest, curiosity and provocation through teachers using the cabinets to set up new collections with items that will provoke children's interest when they see them for the first time. Then they can explore them and use them in follow-up work and provocational investigations.

An outdoor cabinet can be larger and potentially split into different areas. In this way, the outdoor, natural collections that so many children want to share are then given status and a pride of place rather than simply put on a shelf or in a smaller display area. Can you imagine how motivational it would be having your collections displayed in this way if you were four or five years of age?

The indoor cabinet can be a changeable one where you can have set times for when children's collections and items can be displayed and shared and then times when some of the collections listed above can be used. Part of the provocational process can be to let children know when they can bring their things in and then flag up times when it will be your turn to display things. Anticipation is key and will certainly provoke children's interests and curiosity. Who knows where it will lead!

I agree with the brilliant Sue Cowley, who says in her book *The Artful Educator* that the key is to find an object that you find interesting in its own right:

> Sometimes, rather than finding objects that will help you teach a bit of the curriculum, try taking an object that you find interesting in its own right and then figure out what it could help you teach. (Cowley 2017, p.44)

This is at the heart of using provocations and why they work so well with young children. By finding and collecting objects and items that you genuinely find interesting, I guarantee that you will be able to use these in Cabinets of Curiosity and in provocations that spark the curiosity of the children and prompt them in all the right ways. They will be desperate to explore intriguing, unusual collections and more than keen to use them in their learning. Just as Penelope Leach commented, for young children there is no division between play and learning, they learn while living and exploring:

> For a small child there is no division between playing and learning; between the things he or she does just for fun and the things that are educational. The child learns while living and any part of living that is enjoyable is also play. (Leach 2010)

Things to think about

- Have you considered collections in this way before and as a method of provocation?

- What are the practical applications within your setting and classroom?

- Have these things inspired you?

- Can you see the opportunities in including using collections in your long-term planning?

- Would your children react positively to a Cabinet of Curiosity, either indoors or outdoors?

- Who do you think would benefit most from this provocational strategy?

- Have you considered the idea of looking for unique objects before and the role they can play in your practice?

- Could the work of a designer or craftsperson, such as Alexander McQueen, Shaun Leane or Philip Treacy, be used as an effective provocation?

Chapter 7

Small Provocations

Small provocations, those that are either small in size or that are initially designed to only take a small amount of time, can cover all areas of learning and are quick and easy to develop and use. These can be set up simply and be used either in or outdoors and also utilised during more formal 'play-times' or 'break-times' if you share these with older Key Stage 1 children.

Small provocations are just as effective in supporting and developing children's language skills and provide great opportunities for enhancing speaking and listening. This is especially the case if you utilise a 'hidden' or 'secret' element at the start of the provocation where children have to uncover, open or discover the items and resources within a lidded box, or a drawstring bag or mini suitcase. The surprise element intrigues the children, and as a result they quickly become involved in a conversation with the other children they are working with.

Small provocations can also successfully act as a means of supporting specific children in the development of particular schemas and support learning and discovery in areas that they have previously shown a keen interest in. They can also be used as a means of targeting specific development for particular children who may need to revisit an aspect of learning or who may benefit from a supported activity that is more open-ended.

Small provocations can be used effectively when introducing a new theme or aspect of work to a whole class or group of children. From an observation perspective they can provide very valuable information about children's prior knowledge and understanding, and the 'discovery' method provides a great 'get-in' and can help the most reluctant child to want to see what is hidden in a case, box or bag. I've always loved the feeling of not knowing when a new provocation has been left outdoors in the garden or the discovery area. Or when a mysterious case appears in the carpet area inside or on a table, complete with a label and recorded message for the children to discover. TTS (see the Further Resources section at the end of the book) have some excellent resources that can make leaving a message so easy for children to uncover and hear. Talking tin-lids, etc. are so easy to use and can easily be incorporated into a provocation.

An integral element of small provocations is 'loose parts' discovery or manipulative play. Loose parts can be natural or man-made, things that have been found and collected, from the shore or the garden, from the hedgerow or the garage! They can be things that have been grown, dried, painted or polished and increasingly that are upcycled or even bought. We all have our own ways of referring to them and we all have favourite collections and sets of objects that we go back to time and time again. We know the things that fascinate children and the things that will transport individual children to a world where they can manipulate and explore things for hours. Sets and collections of things are an integral part of these small provocations and, with the addition of some other simple resources, the loose part play that you are familiar with can be transformed into a small provocation. The magic happens as children move, manipulate, direct, control and assemble their play with these rich resources, learning as they go and developing their concentration and cooperation.

20 THINGS TO ADD TO TRANSFORM AND PROVOKE

- A mirror tray to place items on
- A coloured plastic or Perspex® box (with a lid if possible)
- A set of clear lights
- A set of single colour or multi-coloured globe lights
- A light box
- A 'write your own message' light, with or without a set word or message
- A neon sign
- A box with a set number of compartments where your loose parts start off
- A set of building cups
- A mixture of coloured ribbon with a loose parts set of items
- A set of small drawstring 'craft' bags
- A collection of clean miniature jam jars with lids
- A set of traditional Russian dolls or stacking dolls
- Empty CD cases
- A small number of material squares
- Egg cups
- A clear sphere that opens
- A number of silk or plastic flowers
- Some tinsel pipe cleaners
- An unusual-shaped box – a star, an octagon, etc.

To add to the provocational element of the resources you are using, add two of the above items and see how the children use them. There really are endless possibilities and ways to construct these small provocations with loose parts. They can link to any area of the curriculum and play a major role in developing concentration, manipulative and fine motor skills, dexterity, early mathematical skills linked to colour and shape, positional vocabulary, scientific knowledge and understanding of properties of materials.

For more examples and ideas to support small provocations, see the Further Resources section.

SMALL PROVOCATIONS AND USEFUL RESOURCES

When you are planning and using small-scale provocations, the one thing you need is a wide selection of resources. Resources are such a vitally important part of using and setting up provocations that getting this right can make everything else fall into place. We all know just how important resources are in the early years classroom and in stimulating the interests and discoveries of four- and five-year-olds.

Sometimes it can be the most unexpected or simplest of items that generate a buzz and a keen interest in young children. Very often children surprise us and relate to the very things we didn't expect. That is why I love using provocations, because despite planning, setting up and anticipating the way things are going to go, you can honestly never really be sure.

Another way to utilise loose parts play in a provocation is to combine two regular elements of your practice. I love working in this way and in surprising the children when they come in at the start of a day or after they have been working somewhere else in the setting. When you are aiming to develop curiosity and the ability to explore within the children, you need to view the resources that you use every day in new and different ways. Water play and sand play are areas in which loose parts can be introduced to great effect. The transformations to provoke are simple and raise questions within the children. They are a source for enhancing and developing discussions and speaking and listening skills.

Here are some ideas that have been very successful and popular with children.

WATER PLAY PROVOCATIONS

- First, only fill the water tray with 1 to 2 cm of water. Take all other regular water play equipment away so that children cannot self-select or add to the provocation. Next select a loose parts collection and add a small number of the items to the water for the children to find, leaving the remaining things on a flat surface adjacent to the water tray. Finally see how the children respond and use the loose parts in the shallow water. If you have a Tuff-Cam, digital camera or iPad that the children are familiar with using, leave this next to the provocation partway through their play and see how they decide to use it.

Adaptations could include:

- Colour the water.

- Add torches in a box and place them under the water tray for the children to find.

- Add natural oils to the water.

- Add lavender hand wash to the water to create bubbles and fragrance.

- Place a thin sheet of material at the bottom of the water tray before adding water, e.g. single colour/multi-coloured/lace pattern/furry/coloured plastic/reflective art paper.

- Place a barrier across the tray separating it into two distinct sections.

- Add a single plastic mirror (or more) or use old CDs.

- Use warm water.

- Use a layer of ice cubes or crushed ice.

- Use play-snow.

- Use cornflour mix.

- Use dried foodstuffs, e.g. rice/polenta/small pasta/ cornflakes. *Note*: always check for allergies to anything children will be in contact with.

The above suggestions can be used with a variety of loose parts collections. All of the selections are intended to encourage curiosity through manipulating things within a medium other than air. This will enable the children to test and trial things and continue to develop their creativity. When I have used these strategies with children in the past, they have loved the unexpected nature of suddenly discovering a different medium in the water tray and have spent extended periods of time exploring the loose part collections in a very different way. It has always raised questions, especially with children who have delayed speech and language skills, as the provocational nature of the 'unfamiliar' has challenged them and elicited in them the sense of awe and wonder.

SAND PLAY AND MALLEABLE PROVOCATIONS

- First, remove the usual sand toys and resources that the children are familiar with. Remove the majority of sand, leaving only a thin 1 to 2 cm layer in the sand tray. As before, select a loose parts collection and place a small number of items in the bottom of the tray area, leaving the remaining items on an adjacent table. Again see how the children respond to these changes and provocations. Add the digital camera, iPad or Tuff-Cam and observe to see if the children record their investigation.

Simple adaptations could include:

- Form a barrier across the sand tray leaving the children with two or four distinct sections to use.

- Use a damp sand solution.

- Use a wet sand solution (with some water still visible).

- Add a small number of very large stones.

- Add a reflective surface under the dry sand/damp/wet sand.

- Replace the sand with another malleable material that the children can manipulate and explore.

- Add Playmobil® or other play figures/superhero action figures/dolls.

If you want to add to your loose parts play cheaply, make regular visits to your local pound shop. They are especially good at seasonal themed resources that can be incorporated into loose parts play, form a new collection or add to an existing one. They are also a great place to ask for contributions from if you are seeking support from parents and carers.

These simple provocations can bring that challenge and excitement back to a familiar learning experience, and as a teacher and practitioner they really make you think. The experience cannot be scripted or rehearsed, you are as much a learner as the children are, and your role is to observe, respond and react to their discovery, exploration and analysis of the situation they find themselves in. You need to be able to have the confidence and patience to wait, observe and then join in with questions and requests the children may ask. You really are working in the role of facilitator and this can be different and at times difficult for some people who have always been at the very centre of things.

Using provocations and provocational learning in this way reminds me of teaching drama and working within the method of Mantle of the Expert, which was originally developed and pioneered by Dorothy Heathcote MBE in the 1960s and 1970s (Heathcote 1984) and has gone on to enable students of all ages to become fully immersed in their learning and develop real understanding of key educational concepts from across the curriculum through working within this way.

Mantle of the Expert is a very specific teaching and learning approach. It is sometimes referred to as a dramatic inquiry approach and assumes a flow of learning where the child is at the centre of things as they take a lead role in the fictional context where they form a 'Company' or collaborative enterprise, where they are commissioned in order to complete an important role for a very important client. Within this, the children are positioned as 'experts' and work in role to complete the job they have been commissioned to carry out by the client. In this way the children have been provoked by the fictional situation they have been introduced to and the inquiry they will engage in. They will be immersed in the learning and will encounter the curriculum in a real-life situation, as opposed to within separate 'subjects' or 'aspects', just as early years children will encounter things within provocations. In each distinct approach to learning, the children are at the centre of the experience as the teacher starts from the children's interests and needs alongside specific curriculum objectives. The children then use their prior knowledge of all aspects of the curriculum to discover and build new learning. This will not simply come from one area of the curriculum, or cover one area of interest for a child, but will cover numerous areas, enabling all children to learn collaboratively from each other and to develop key speaking and listening skills throughout their engagement.

⠶Ǭ⠶ Things to think about

- What do I think of small provocations and loose parts play?

- Could they add value to my classroom and children?

- Could I use small provocations to develop specific aspects of learning in my setting?

- What additional resources would I need to help me in this?

- In what ways would small provocations support my enabling environment?

- Consider the ways Mantle of the Expert could support your practice in the classroom.

- Do you need to find out more about Mantle of the Expert?

Chapter 8

Longer Provocations

Some provocations can last much longer than just one session or one day. Here are some areas of the early years setting or classroom that we may have overlooked regarding their provocational purposes: the role-play area, the reading area/corner or class library, our writing areas and art spaces and workshops. In these areas we tend to plan for a theme for a while, select our resources, plan how we will start with them, set up, introduce them to the children and leave the rest to them.

As early years practitioners and teachers, we are very familiar with planning long-term schemes of work for our role-play areas and with revising and updating our reading and writing areas on a regular basis. There are some superb examples of how role-play areas can be transformed into stunning enabling areas that promote discovery, learning, high levels of self-discovery and symbolic play. With the onset of outdoor 'kitchens', we increasingly see this in the outdoor learning of our children too. Through re-focusing our thinking and planning, we can introduce the element of provocation into these areas and see additional benefits and development across the whole curriculum.

An example of this would be the development of the role-play area into a bookshop with a stage area incorporated into it. The regular roles of bookseller, shop owner, shelf stocker, delivery person and customers would all be catered for and the children could take part in these as you would expect. However, the element of provocations take place when at some point in each day a letter is opened in the shop that gives a problem or a difficult scenario to solve. The roles the children then have to play and explore become more specific and are directly in response to the 'provocation' that was delivered in the letter. Information could also be given via a Skype-type message, a Facetime call or a delivery from the school admin assistant or school secretary. The daily challenges enable the children to stretch their imagination and understanding and solve real-life situations.

With the addition of a 'stage' development area within the bookshop and a table and tuff tray, additional provocations can be suggested to coincide with particular books that are being explored in class, and with particular characters from the stories. These can be further developed via the stage area/tuff trays with block and small world resources, all adding to the children's development and understanding of character, setting, motive, etc. Roles can be allocated for children, so that they are introduced to real-life roles related to producing books. They can be storytellers, researchers, authors, illustrators, publishers, graphic designers, publicists, booksellers and anyone else working with books. Children will naturally want to explore these roles if they are introduced in fun and creative ways. Teachers can play a specific role to enhance and develop the children's learning by using the teaching method 'Teacher in Role'. By acting 'in role' and using, for example, the ideas outlined in job adverts posted in the shop, children can be engaged in discussions, asked questions, and so on. Children love to build on things, and if you can build in visits from a children's author or illustrator during the time of the longer provocation, it will help to support the learning and extend the children's understanding. Children's authors love to come to school, and lesser-known authors benefit from being able to share their work with a wider number of children. Don't just restrict the visits to book authors; children love poets – who is more successful and adored when he visits schools than

Michael Rosen? Why not invite an illustrator or graphic novelist into school, or someone who works in book publishing? They will all add to the children's understanding and make for a memorable learning experience.

When planning these events myself, I have linked with other local schools so that we can share the cost; if you are a member of a network of academies this can work very well and lead to shared follow-up work. This worked particularly well when we invited Michael Rosen to visit one school that I worked in. Never ask an author to visit school for free – this is their work and they need to be paid for their time and the visit. However, the benefits of an author visit are immeasurable and the benefits will be far-reaching. I've included some people you may want to consider in the Further Resources section at the back of the book.

When you walk into an early years setting it is usual to see an art area with familiar resources and equipment that we are all familiar with – a painting section, a cutting and sticking section, printing, drawing with different mark-making items, modelling area with dough and malleable materials to select from and a good paper selection. If you are wondering where the provocations come into things, here goes: the key is to change things up!

PAINTING AREA

If you know you've had one aspect for one area of art covered for a few weeks, change things! It's so easy to have the same type of painting out and we have all fallen into that trap. I know I have. We know the children are familiar with it, they know where everything is and can use that knowledge to paint things related to what your key areas of focus are and that makes everyone's life easier. The simplest way to include a provocation in an already established painting area is to change the type of painting you are setting up and asking the children to do. So, move from ready mix paint in spiltop cups to block paints; this requires the children to generate the paint for themselves and gives them time to think before they actually add anything to paper. Put out a range of brushes too and reduce the number of colours so that the children have to use their colour mixing knowledge to make the other colours that aren't there. It's simple, but it does provoke a new interest in the area, which should encourage different children to explore it, and it promotes thinking as not all the colours are simply there to use.

Other simple ways to do this are:

- Set up watercolour sets and see how the children respond.

- Use a combination of types of paint – block paint and watercolour, or ready mixed paint in primary colours and watercolour in secondary colours.

- Set up the painting areas with only black, white and one other colour plus water, changing the one other colour every other day.

- Use oil-based paint.

- Use pearlised paint with a range of colours, then change the colour combinations as above over a week or two.

- Set up only shades of one colour in different paint types and rotate the colour used.

If your usual method of painting takes place on a large flat table, introduce easels for a period of time and see how the children use them and how this alters their painting work. Then after a period of free exploration, use the strategies from above to provoke re-exploration.

This should also be done outdoors and is a good structure to use across a set period of time. When working in the outdoors, add to the provocation by getting the children to develop their own methods for adding paint to paper by removing brushes at certain times and setting the challenge to find outdoor items to use instead. Grass, twigs, leaves and combinations of all three make wonderful paint implements and add to the children's ability to explore the paint and representation.

DRAWING AREA

The same things can be done with drawing, printing and malleable work. I'm also a huge believer in the power of moving your areas to achieve maximum effect. One key aspect of provocations is to do just this. If your children are expecting the drawing or mark-making area to be in a certain place, change it. Change the location and the size and shape of the table layout. Giving more room or utilising a corner with wall space can make a huge difference to the way an area feels and also to the number of children who go to access this. In addition, by altering the established way the resources are stored, you can provoke different responses and encourage children to use unfamiliar materials and so increase their mark-making and drawing skills.

- Just as before, change from table-based to easel-based work for a week or two (this improves children's strength in their hands, arms, shoulders and back, leading to greater fine motor control in readiness for writing).

- Only use pencil crayons for a week.

- Then use wax crayons.

- Next use felt tips.

- Then coloured biro-type pens.

- Now combine two forms the children have used before (e.g. pencil and biro pens).

- Set up the area with soft pastel crayons.

- Use fountain pens and feather quills with coloured inks.

- Use glitter and pearlescent pens.

- Only use marker pens and larger-sized chubby crayons.

- Set up mixed boxes, but with colour limitations as you did with paint.

- Set up boxes with shades of one colour.

- Add books with very specific styles of drawing.

- Add a book from a particular artist.

- Include laminated postcards of a subject you want the children to explore.

- Put up a wall-based display ready for the start of a new week in the drawing area and link the pens/pencils/ crayons, etc. to the colours in the display.

- Use film or book posters to provoke children's drawing skills and their end products.

- Fill a lidded box with small anatomical artist's models. Put an 'open' sign on the box. Place this in the middle of the table and set out a range of drawing pencils (HB, B, B4, B6, B8, H2, H4) and see what the provocation results in.

- Load a digital photograph frame with images that link to work you are doing and have it on the table.

- Use a talking tin lid or recording device to give instructions for what to do.

- Remember to change the paper choice, size, colour and shape to provoke an interest and response.

- Get children to draw using naturally found materials.

- Use gathered materials from Forest Schools or outdoor sessions.

- Have a drawing materials amnesty and ask parents and families to donate things they no longer use; set these up and use for the area.

PRINTING AREA

As with the other distinct areas related to art, the printing area benefits from the use of provocations. Change things up as suggested in the earlier section with the art area and painting. Have you ever set up printing on an easel or series of easels? Have you used large cotton sheets or long scarf-style strips of material for children to print on? Have the children made banners or outdoor flags? Have they printed t-shirts or designed wallpaper, wrapping paper, socks, cushions, carpets or reusable shopping bags?

With the development of printing skills, provocations can be quickly and easily introduced by using limited colour palettes at particular times and exploring different types of printing materials and shapes to print on.

Ask children to donate their old PE shoes and use these to print patterns on. Envelopes donated from local card stores or stationers and shoe boxes make excellent spaces to print on too.

One of the most rewarding and effective forms of printing is Batik. Batik can be seen as a dyeing technique, but essentially the process involves adding or printing dots and lines to create the pattern with the resist using a copper stamp called a cap. Batik is a beautiful thing to do and links art work to cultural understanding and craftsmanship. In October 2009 UNESCO designated Indonesian Batik as a Masterpiece of Oral and Intangible Heritage of Humanity. If you can get someone to come into your class and demonstrate, the impact and results are stunning. Young children are fascinated by the process and love to explore it once they have seen how it works. This is definitely something that can be used to produce high-quality end products that can be taken home and treasured. T-shirts, bookmarks, book bags and scarves are all simply printed and produced.

Once children are familiar with a range of printing techniques, you can begin to explore the myriad of possibilities and provocations via traditional patterns from all over the world. Islamic art and traditional tile patterns from Portugal are stunning examples that can be used in provocations and as major stimuli for the children to develop their own work from. The art curriculum requires children to explore and understand the work of local craftspeople, and traditional pattern work can be explored and used as a means of provocation. The work of William Morris, Charles Rennie Macintosh and Margaret Macdonald can be explored, and local galleries and museums can provide information regarding work from your local area. This is also an excellent way to develop children's knowledge and understanding of colour, pattern, shape, sequence, tessellation, symmetry and rotation in a creative and cross-curricular way.

MALLEABLE AREA

With the malleable area we probably usually think of using playdough, soft stuff, plasticine or clay – these kinds of materials enable the children to manipulate, build strength in their fingers, hands and wrists, and develop creativity and concentration. I would hazard a guess that we don't associate cooking with this area of the classroom and would very rarely put them together. Here is one really simple way in which we can provoke the children's interests, excite them and enhance a whole range of skills and knowledge at the same time.

Change your malleable area into a cooking zone for a half term and use it every day. I know you're already thinking 'but this is a huge resource implication, both for staff and for daily resources', and I agree, but the benefits will outweigh any difficulties in that direction. If a half term is just too long for you, commit to a shorter period of time. You will still see so many changes and the children will gain so much. This can be developed in a number of ways, and when I have seen this in practice or done it myself, a few things have always taken place beforehand. You can simply decide to remove your malleable resources, set up your new 'kitchen' area for baking or making, and let the children explore. If this really isn't for you, or you feel your children aren't ready for this (and this could be down to the stage in the academic year or the children's developmental stages), start off with something they have already experienced as part of a teacher-led activity. They might have decorated shop-bought biscuits and you could leave all the known ingredients and resources to enable them to decorate, plus some additional things to extend their learning, and start there. You could follow this up with making sandwiches using a variety of bread, buns and fillings, then moving on to individual pizzas using readymade pizza dough. To extend the provocational nature, adapt the range of ingredients throughout the week by adding or taking one away and by introducing other utensils and implements such as sandwich-shaped cutters and ingredients in sealed tubs or jars. These are just a few things you could do:

- Sandwiches
- Fruit kebabs
- Pizza
- Cakes
- Biscuits

- Bread

- Salad

When the children are familiar with the area and have explored food that they know, introduce a fantasy element with a café sign announcing what is to be made for the day such as Unicorn bites and add tubs of Fluff, edible glitter and cake decorations, with cake stands to display them on! Make huge traybakes of sponge cake in a separate session and use the finished trays to let the children cut slices of cakes from and make into cake kebabs. Once they have made bread, leave the ingredients and see if they can replicate the process and leave cheese or dried fruit to be included in their final batches. I was lucky and worked with some very understanding and totally fun cooks and kitchen managers who were more than happy to be involved in some 'acting in role', who would come in and ask my children to make some fruit kebabs or salad bowls or pizza for lunch. This was always such a fantastic way of provoking even more involvement and the development of 'something special' for lunch.

Another provocation could be arranging for your children to make snacks or a special lunch for another class, or parents or members of the community.

Quick changes to provoke in the malleable area:

- Add Modroc and let the children explore.

- Then add material to frame the Modroc – chicken wire/ wooden or plastic weaving frames/bubble wrap/silver foil/cardboard and plastic containers.

- Investigate new craft materials and things that you have not used before and include these.

- Leave pre-cut square clay tiles and clay tools. Air-dry clay is excellent for this.

- Playfoam.

- Modelling boards.

- Ice-cream dough.

As with any work in this area, check for allergies and any items that children should not be exposed to either on health or other safety grounds. Always make sure that they have access to water and hand wash to make sure hands are fully clean when handling any kind of food and keep floor and surfaces slip-free.

DEVELOPMENT OF THE WORKSHOP/ CONSTRUCTION AREA

I always loved changing up the construction area and making it into a 'Workshop Zone' complete with realistic signs, instructions, data and health and safety notices. Many of these things can be older, outdated health and safety notices that are regularly sent into schools, and a letter or social media request to local businesses and garages usually results in some really useful materials that can make this provocation really work.

As with other areas, the key is to make it as inviting as possible, and if the initial 'big change' for the provocation can take place over a holiday and the children return to find something totally new, all the better.

The addition of workshop overalls or lab-style jackets (that can be found on the TTS website – see Further Resources) can add to the provocation and also entice children who may not readily select construction-style activities.

The inclusion of other 'Key Jobs' makes for further exploration and creativity and enables children to make connections to other areas of work they know about.

Telephones, fax machines, tool kits, job sheets, invoices and credit cards and chip and pin machines all contribute to the reality of the provocation once the construction materials are included. These can be a smaller selection of things that the children are already familiar with or the introduction of a new set of items. The aim is to keep the reality element of the 'Workshop', and so restricting the construction items works best. Better still if these can be woven into another aspect of the children's themed work where they can further explore areas. Perhaps the 'Workshop' could be building something to use in the outdoors or fix the baking and cooking utensils needed for the food area?

The inclusion of outdoor wooden blocks and pipes can also be another added element to the 'Workshop'. Emails can arrive telling the team that they are to be visited by a safety inspector and customers can come to pay and find they have left their credit card at home. Real-life scenarios used as part of the longer-term provocation make every day a little different and extend the learning and discovery in a fun and creative way which actively supports other aspects of learning, including maths, science, language and communication.

:Q: Things to think about

- What things would I like to try from the above ideas?

- Can I use provocations in my role-play area? Could I use the 'bookshop' idea or develop a similar concept to extend the children's learning and creative skills?

- What specific dispositions, attitudes and skills would a provocation of this kind develop within the children?

- Could you initiate any of the adaptations in your art area? Would they support your children's learning? In what ways?

Chapter 9

Themed Provocations

I absolutely love themed provocations. They are a joy to plan and hen to watch as the children become engrossed in them and develop them in their own unique ways, reflecting their ideas and passions, exploring situations, sharing, discovering and learning so many things. Whenever I have been involved in them I have always found them to be so rewarding and, let's be honest, we all need that in our daily working lives. The inspiration that other themed provocations can bring is one of the great things about having a network of early years practitioners. Hearing of other provocations can give you a spark of inspiration and support your planning and practice too. I never get tired of hearing about the work that other people are doing and hope that the provocations in this book will bring the same kind of inspiration to you.

One of the most recent themed provocations I have heard of was shared via Twitter by Jan Dubiel, who is an independent Early Years Advisor and former Head of National and International Development at Early Excellence. It was developed in a nursery in Bristol and was based around the theme of the Glastonbury Festival. It featured on the BBC News website in July 2019. The article and video reported that the staff at the nursery wanted to create a Glastonbury experience for their children and 'bring Glastonbury to us'. With the huge number of applications for tickets, most children will never experience the festival themselves, and as a themed provocation, it's outstanding. I wish

I had thought of it! Every child needed a special VIP wristband to go to the festival, where there was a festival campsite with child-sized pop-up tents, quiet garden areas, face painting to add to the authentic experience, a yoga area with yoga mats and yoga teaching, a main stage area for the performances and of course portaloos! The children 'headlined' the festival, singing, playing instruments and dancing, and had been involved in the developing and building of the areas, including making the wristbands, the portaloos and the main stage area. As Jan Dubiel commented in the discussion following his initial post, this was a genuine version of developing cultural capital for all of these children as it was 'providing alternative experiences to broaden their world view' (Jan Dubiel, July 2019)

Now what I want to know is, what happened next? Did the festival experience grow? Were there poetry and story readings? Did the children make and sell street food from all over the world? Was there a circus tent or performers, meditation times? Could the children sit and relax by watching a favourite film in the cinema area? Could they make puppets, play with giant balloons and design and make their own festival t-shirts? Did they learn about caring for the environment and climate change and why Glastonbury had gone plastic-free in 2019 after using, and recycling, 40 tonnes of plastic bottles in 2017 and composting 132 tonnes of food waste? Whatever the answers are to my questions, I know these children learned so much from their Glastonbury experience. They are a total inspiration.

A memorable themed provocation that took place in my own Reception/Year 1 classroom happened completely by chance. It wasn't pre-planned, or even thought of. It happened as the result of an off-the-cuff comment I made to my class late one dark winter's evening when we needed to have every light on in the room simply to see what we were doing. The weather was dark and brooding as the increasingly dark afternoons drew in as we rapidly raced towards the Christmas break. We were knee deep in the usual hectic and gloriously slightly 'off balance' run of activities that every primary school teacher and their class are familiar with. With that in mind, with clock ticking towards 3:30 pm, there were a number of tired faces, grumbles and giggles as we tried in vain to find the right number of tables and chairs that were usually in our classroom.

We were fortunate enough to be in a lovely new building where the two Reception classes shared a beautiful double open plan unit that led out onto a sizable enclosed quad where we had a range of outdoor equipment and resources, including raised beds for planting and some well-established trees and plants. Between both rooms we had a special tucked-away space called a keiva, an area and concept that originated in Scandinavian schools. This additional space enabled us to utilise this area for a whole range of different things throughout the year. I remember a couple of children asking to go and check if the chairs were 'hiding in the keiva', and that's when it happened. I said, 'Oh, the chair monster must have eaten them.' And there it was, the provocation. I thought nothing of it until 30 seconds later when the children came running across the classroom (which they just wouldn't have normally done) shouting, 'The chairs have gone, they've gone, the chair monster must have eaten them!' In that split second something slightly magical occurred within the room. Other children began to realise something had happened, or was happening: some stopped tidying things away, some came over to where I stood with the children who had made the discovery, some carried on with their tasks, while others just listened to what was going on. The atmosphere had shifted – I knew it, and so did the children. I could choose to squash it and concentrate on getting ready for the end of the day or I could grasp it, capitalise upon it and run with it. So that's what I did, letting the children take the lead and carry on with their excited conversation. By the time we were ready to go home the class had decided that I needed to warn the caretaker and ask them to let them know if they had seen anything unusual or suspicious.

As they left for the end of the day, meeting parents and grandparents, friends and people from other classes, the excited chatter was of lost chairs, things going missing and a chair monster!

I have to confess that I underestimated the power of my throwaway comment and the subsequent, somewhat rushed and excited discussion that took place at the end of the day. However, by 9:00 am the following morning there was no underestimating what had happened overnight and the impact of one of those magical 'Spark' moments that make teaching and being in an early years classroom a total and utter joy.

The classroom doors were opened at 8:50 am every morning. At 8:40 am that morning I was fending off little knocks on the doors and children asking if they could come in early, count the chairs, talk to the caretaker and making somewhat nervous enquiries regarding if I had seen the chair monster! I rapidly re-evaluated what I was going to do for the first part of the morning and realised that something quite special had happened overnight.

When one of my Reception children arrived clutching a huge stack of A4 sheets of paper and proceeded to ask if I would read her story about the chair monster and show everyone her drawings, I realised we were on to something! Fourteen sheets of A4 paper later, a totally enthralled class, a huge number of questions and a promise to read the story again at home time, and my planned day began. The thing was that whatever I had on paper at that time wasn't very valuable, either to me as a teacher or to my children. They were consumed by questions, ideas, theories and quietly excited chatter. I realised that I had to have the courage of my convictions and be brave enough to take my mentor's advice and go to Plan B. There was a whole treasure trove of unexplored learning right within the grasp of my amazing class and I had to be confident enough to 'go with it'. So that's what I did. One rather frantic planning session for the remainder of the day took place during break time (when I wasn't on duty), and my remaining sessions were based around the now notorious chair monster and the amazingly creative work that had been produced, at home, by one of the girls in my class.

That was really when the fun started and the exploration of this surprise idea took off. The children needed to talk and explore their ideas, theories and questions regarding the chair monster, and so we held a whole class discussion where I simply facilitated. I wrote down all of their ideas and questions and we used this discussion as a basis for their independent work. I was surprised by the intensity of the talk, the vocabulary that the children were using and that some of the usually more reticent children were taking the lead. To see the children's confidence and enthusiasm grow throughout the morning was a total joy and gave me one of those teaching moments that you tuck away and treasure.

I based the next few weeks' teaching and learning around the 'chair monster' concept and the children's theories that were generated in the first discussion session. If I'd planned for ten years I simply would not have been able to come up with the varied and creatively driven ideas that my class came up with. All aspects of learning were covered and developed and without any contrived shoe-horning of concepts that can at times take place. The learning genuinely came from the children's ideas and gave a huge sense of personal ownership to the children. The pace within sessions was at times too fast as some children wanted to race ahead with their personal ideas, and their brains were reacting to earlier work so quickly that the days were often just not long enough!

You could argue that what I did after the initial 'idea' took off was nothing to do with provocations at all. Well, I agree. But it was a perfect opportunity to go with the children's obvious, very enthusiastic interests, just as Reggio Emilia recommends. I had some very reluctant writers, talkers and children who found collaborative work very difficult. With this it all seemed to melt away; any teacher would have done what I did. I'm glad I did. It was memorable for the children but also memorable for me. I remember it so clearly even after so many years and after working in six other schools. I still believe that creative opportunities need to be grabbed with both hands. When children are learning that fast and dictating the pace, don't fight it, go with it and help them to discover! I'm glad I did.

Morecambe Bay School case study

I first became aware of Morecambe Bay School when a local news item featured a story about a Lancashire school that had used Tim Peake's time on the European Space Station as a stimulus and provocation for their work. At the time so many schools were doing just the same, and I must admit that I thought it was just another such story; lovely for the school to be featured, fabulous for the children and their families, but not unique. Good for them, I thought, as I half listened to the report. The following day they were on my local TV news round-up at 6:30 pm and the story had taken a dramatic turn of events. By the following morning children from the school were being interviewed by the BBC on their national news programmes, and articles in national newspapers and the *TES* followed.[1] This wasn't an ordinary feel-good school story. It was so much more. This project, with provocations at its core, turned from a long-term science project to something that no one at the school could ever have imagined. With the national media coverage, in both newspapers and on television, the school's work became an overnight talking point across the country and the children truly experienced a life-changing

---

1   https://www.independent.co.uk/news/science/find-sam-toy-dog-missing-space-morecambe-bay-burnley-a6973641.html

learning experience. From that moment I've been intrigued by the school and their philosophy and how this matches with the use of provocations for learning, not only in the early years, but also throughout the whole school.

I'm delighted to say that their headteacher, Siobhan Collingwood, is a wonderful advocate of provocational learning and is happy to discuss her philosophy and ethos if you wish to contact her. I am planning to visit the school in the future and personally cannot wait to see the wonderful school.

Paul Brown and outdoor learning provocations

I have been lucky enough to be a colleague and friend of Paul for over 20 years. I worked with his wife in my second school and have learned so much from working with him, sharing ideas, being involved in joint projects and in finding our feet in headship together. Everyone needs someone like Paul in their lives.

Paul and I have both worked in a diverse range of primary schools throughout our careers, many in socially deprived areas with diverse needs, where children's life experiences have been limited in some ways. The predominant driving force has always been to provide a rich, creative curriculum, where firsthand experiences engender memorable learning opportunities that children will not only learn from but remember.

There are so many things I could include in this book about Paul and the work he has done in schools, many that adhere to using provocations in learning. For example, planning and installing purpose-built themed reading areas (to promote reading and a love of books in every classroom from early years to Year 6), with themes such as a pirate ship, a rainforest, a castle and a cave. But the one I discussed with him is a unique outdoor learning provocation that was built around the aim of developing social skills for all children and that enabled older and younger children to learn and work together.

AN OUTDOOR PROVOCATION OF ENORMOUS PROPORTIONS!

I remember going to visit Paul when the idea of the outdoor area was in its infancy. I had recently completed a two-year outdoor learning building project that incorporated a large-scale musical instrument trail that led children from our outdoor adventure play areas in one part of the school grounds, past our reading circle complete with talking tubes, through a wooded secret garden area to the early years area where we had just completed 'the dragonfly learning area', which was a unique, outdoor classroom where all aspects of the curriculum could be taught 365 days a year. We had installed an enormous canopied sand area, fixed water play troughs, a stage and outdoor literacy area, an early years-sized climbing frame and slide, sculptures, a wooden statues space for an outdoor learning tepee, seated areas, quiet zones, over-sized chalk boards for signs and mark-making, planters, tubs and permanent wellie stores! We were both excited to see the effects the developments would have on our children and their learning. We both wanted to motivate our children to become independent learners who could access the curriculum in many ways.

The one thing we were certain of was that we did not want the traditional experience of children going outside at play times to a blank playground with little to do and nowhere to go. We were determined to provide things that grabbed the children's attention, motivated them and provoked their play and learning. Paul had an area to the side of his recently refurbished Early Years Unit that was crying out for attention. He was passionate about inclusion, outdoor learning and Forest Schools and wanted to provide another space where multi-layered play could take place and where children of all ages could access the space at particular times. Together with the teaching staff, he wanted to create a space where less confident children could also sit and observe the play and join in when they were ready. Part of the objective was to support the language development of the children and to give them an area that would promote (and provoke) talk and discussion. A huge hill was created, with a tunnel space built in to create a cave section where children could play, explore and use a variety of equipment. Enormous 'Stonehenge'-style structures were secured over and adjacent to the hill area and grass was re-laid over the hill with sand forming the floor area of the henge. The structure enabled children to engage in both large-scale adventurous play and small world play with the use of figures and associated equipment. At times traditional sand toys, wheeled toys and resources for volume and capacity were used. The area was used throughout the day by the EYFS children and at lunch and break times by a mixture of other ages, enabling children across all key stages to interact, play and develop together.

The area also provided a fabulous provocation for imaginative, creative play and provided an on-site provocation for cross-curricular writing, art work, maths, science, history and geography development. In many ways the only limitation on its use was that of the imagination of the children and the ideas of the teachers.

☼ Things to think about

- How do you feel about themed provocations?

- What is your reaction to the 'bring Glastonbury to us' provocation?

- Would you consider developing a festival-themed provocation in your setting?

- How do you think your children would react to the provocation?

- What would your fellow teachers' reactions be if you suggested this?

- Have you ever been involved in a longer-term provocation as in the examples in this chapter?

Chapter 10

The Power of Books as Provocations

Books of all kinds can be used as excellent provocations, not only in the early years but in other year groups too. By now you will probably have gathered that I am a book fan, or book worm, or reading fanatic – whatever you want to call me is absolutely OK. I adore books and the power they have to transform learning, to instil a million emotions, enable children to live other lives and step in so many other people's shoes, both in the present and from the past. They are a treasure for so many reasons. One of my favourite book quotes is:

A library is a hospital for the mind. (Anonymous)

One of the most beautiful and heartfelt provocations I have seen was based around the use of a picture book. Not a traditional preschool, brightly coloured and loud picture book, but an exquisite, wordless, sepia-paged book by Shaun Tan called *The Arrival* (Tan 2007). I was first introduced to it when I attended the Power of Reading training organised by the Centre for Literacy in Primary Education. The book has a quiet, haunting quality and almost feels like an artefact. The book was used with a mixed class of Year 5 and 6 children. The impact it had upon them – their depth of discussion, analysis, growth in empathy and understanding about the human condition – was a joy to behold. From a teaching point of view the book had provoked the strongest reactions from the class and was one of the most memorable pieces of work I have had the pleasure to be involved in. If you don't know the book, or the author, I'd encourage you to take a look and discover how his books can be used as beautiful provocations. They can be used with all age ranges and I'm sure you will return to them time and time again.

If you are keen to meet other people who have a passion for using books and quality children's literature in the classroom, investigate ReadingRocks via Twitter and their website (see Further Resources at the end of the book) and be inspired by Simon Smith, who is a huge advocate of how important books are in children's learning. Simon Smith is headteacher at a Yorkshire primary school and regularly contributes to conferences. He is a regular supplier of brilliant suggestions for books that can be used not only for provocations, but for all other aspects of learning, and particularly to develop a child's love of reading. How wonderful is that?

I am a huge advocate of immersing young children in books and reading. I think that can be the most powerful form of provocation there is. Someone used the term 'drown them in books and reading' recently; I thought it was perfect. There was no doubt about what they meant. I'm all in favour of that. I think I'd like to be at their school.

Far too many children at the present time view reading as a thing to tick off, or to make sure they get a particular score on. They are well versed in practising for and passing tests, their phonic training is excellent and they can de-code. But reading, books and literature are so much more than that. They always have been and always should be. By using books in a provocational context and to stimulate and support holistic learning throughout the curriculum, or indeed to focus children upon one very specific area of life and understanding as Shaun Tan's book does, we are building an openness, a love of discovery, an empathy and understanding of things beyond the children's everyday existence that can bring the wider world into their hands. That is a key element of what is required by the Foundation Stage Curriculum and also the National Curriculum. Books really are instrumental in delivering this.

I have used many of the books below within my teaching and have used them as a provocation. Some books have also been used as a basis for Philosophy for Children (P4C) sessions, which are also a means of provoking interest, understanding and discovery for children from a very early age (see later in this chapter).

GENERAL BOOK LIST

- *Who's Hiding at the Seaside?* by Katherine McEwen
- *Brenda Is a Sheep* by Morag Hood
- *The Quiet Crocodile Goes to the Beach* by Natacha Andriamirado
- *The Way to Treasure Island* by Lizzy Stewart
- *Through the Eyes of Us* by Jon Roberts
- *Tooth Fairy in Training* by Michelle Robinson
- *Boy Oh Boy* by Cliff Leek
- *Cherry Moon* by Zaro Well
- *A Mouse Called Julian* by Joe Todd-Stanton
- *Fanatical about Frogs* by Owen Davey
- *Kind* by Alison Green, illustrated by Axel Scheffler
- *Stephano the Squid Hero of the Deep* by Wendy Meddour
- *The Incredible Ecosystems of Planet Earth* by Rachel Ignotofsky
- *What Do Machines Do All Day?* by Jo Nelson
- *A Moon Girl Stole My Friend* by Rebecca Patterson
- *Circle* by Mac Barnett

PHILOSOPHY FOR CHILDREN BOOKS

So many books can be used for P4C. You really only need to have a book that raises questions or has a strong discussion point, something that the children can generate a question from and develop from there.

Here are some that you might like to try:

- *Why Are There so Many Bears?* by Kristina Stephenson
- *A Child of Books* by Oliver Jeffers
- *The Missing Book Shop* by Katie Clapham
- *Time for Bed, Miyuki* by Roxane Marie Galliez and Seng Soun Ratanavanh
- *Flat Cat* by Hiawyn Oram
- *A Lion in the Meadow* by Margaret Mahy
- *Albert* by Lani Yamamoto
- *Charlotte's Piggy Bank* by David McKee
- *Clocks and More Clocks* by Pat Hutchins
- *Frog and the Birdsong* by Max Velthuijs
- *Frog and the Stranger* by Max Velthuijs
- *The Giving Tree* by Shel Silverstein
- *Home in the Sky* by Jeannie Baker
- *Not Now, Bernard* by David McKee
- *Planet of the Bears* by Giles Andreae
- *Poems for Thinking* by Robert Fisher
- *Q is for Question* by Tiffany Poirier
- *The Dance of Wallowy Bigness* by Giles Andreae
- *The Garden* by Dyan Sheldon and Gary Blythe

USING PHILOSOPHY FOR CHILDREN AS A PROVOCATION

I have used P4C for over 20 years, and from the moment I heard about this way of working I was a dedicated advocate. It is a unique way of working and, despite 'philosophy' being a scary word, particularly when we consider using it with our youngest children in early years, it is a wonderful way to enable all children to participate and find their voice, to share their ideas about the world and life and to consider other people's point of view.

I am now lucky enough to be working with Cumbria Development Education Centre, a small charity which works with schools across Cumbria and Lancashire. Part of their work is to support schools and teachers in the development of P4C. I am also involved in developing and piloting a new project for the development of children's wellbeing and positive mental health through the use of P4C. It is an exciting time and a project I am very proud of.

P4C not only engages children with a range of books, as they can be used for the initial stimulus or provocation, but it provides children with a safe environment to explore complex questions and ideas, emotions, feelings and morals, and share and learn from others within the community of enquiry.

P4C puts enquiry at the heart of the children's learning and is a form of provocation in that the material used, whether that is a picture book, early story book, photograph or artefact, will provoke thought and raise questions. P4C actively helps to develop children's personal and group self-esteem, intellectual confidence and speaking and listening skills, and enables them to contribute to their school-based community and, ultimately, society. Children also make connections, respect others' beliefs and opinions, formulate questions, learn to reflect, cooperate and collaborate, and challenge, explore and develop their own views.

The process is totally inclusive, with the community of enquiry always being formed into a circle, enabling all children and adults participating at a mutual level where everyone can see and make eye contact with everyone else. A pupil vote forms a key part of the enquiry process and reinforces the democratic process and always ends with a period of reflection and debrief. Each session brings something new and is always totally rewarding. It is another form of provocation that can be sensitively and gradually introduced to young children over a period of time and used to support and develop their learning in many ways.

If you are interested in developing this within your setting, I would encourage you to observe some P4C enquiries and attend some training. You won't look back.

:💡: **Things to think about**

- What could my children gain from using a more diverse range of books that provoke?

- Do I need to extend the range of books I use in the classroom?

- Do I have enough examples of new authors and writers?

- Could I use P4C in my classroom?

- Do I need to find out more about P4C and how I could use it?

Chapter 11

The Power of Messages

Messages of all kinds can be a powerful tool for provocations. They are the perfect way to capture the imagination of children at the start of a new area of work. Whether written or recorded, messages have a power to transform children's learning through provocations.

As we have covered the creative aspect in the art area (see Chapter 8), it makes sense to further expand upon how the power of a very specific message 'in character' can be used as a provocation and ultimately motivate the children and their learning. This can also have the additional advantage of resulting in related learning and discovery taking place at home and has been utilised in strategies that we are all familiar with such as Barnaby Bear in Geography and home-time toys such as 'wise owl' or Story Bear.

Young children love to be included in creative and imaginative play, and when this is implicit and shared with the teacher it can be a very powerful thing. Shared experiences and ownership heighten the importance for children and they feel a real desire to support and develop the play. That is why repetitive stories with strong characters work so well in early years (and indeed older ages – Harry Potter is an excellent example of this, with the repetition of key characters and plot devices). The use of written provocations such as letters, messages, notes or emails is very effective at starting a longer-term provocation as they set the scene and initiate a shared feeling of ownership and involvement.

This strategy relates directly to the letters in traditional tales that young children become so familiar with, either through listening to the stories or having the stories read to them. Once children are familiar with the plot device of a letter in these stories, they can work with great effect within the classroom and be used as a key tool to hook children in and drive learning forward through the means of provocation.

I have personally used this method many, many times and have always found that it intrigues the children and demands that they ask more. It is an excellent way of introducing a situation where the children have to take an active role in something and can be tailored to meet the needs of any aspect of the curriculum. It also places the teacher in a different role as the letter, message, etc. is not from them and so they become part of the learning journey and act in a separate role from the usual one they take within the classroom. This can result in the children being more decisive and motivated to take a lead in the work as they feel it is coming from a different direction and not simply from the teacher. This in itself can result in children who do not normally take a leading role in things having a newfound confidence to do so. The power dynamic within the classroom changes and the children quickly pick up upon this. From the moment the letter is addressed to them and read to them, they have the responsibility to do what is requested and required. Young children take responsibility seriously and want to be in charge. We see this frequently when they role play home situations and want to be the adults or older members of the family. The use of letters as provocations draws upon this, enabling them to fulfil these desires to 'role play' adult roles, make decisions, drive things forward and take control.

A good strategy with letters is to ask for help or for the children to solve some sort of problem. Taking on a specific task or role is also very effective and can then relate to other necessary learning and exploration taking place in order to complete the request. Obviously this can relate to any aspect of the curriculum, as stated before, and this can also be used in relation to community-based learning and activities that are pertinent to your specific school and locality. If we relate this back to art, and how letters can be used as a provocational device, a letter can be used to stretch children's art techniques, to link to a specific artist or stimulus and provide the challenge for everyone to develop their skills.

Be bold when using the provocation of a letter. Let it have status and importance, as this will grab the children's attention and hold their interest. If you can involve someone well known by the children, even better. Some of the best provocations are the boldest, and how wonderful is it to be immersed in that world for young children? Notes and letters from favourite book characters and super heroes, or role-play characters that are used regularly in school, such as 'take-home bear' or the teacher next door, can all work really well. You may decide upon a letter to the class from the town's Mayor, who has been told that the school have been learning about a particular artist perhaps or local event. The Mayor has been let down by a group who were supposed to provide art work for the Town Hall. Can the children help with this situation? Can they help to solve the Mayor's problem? Remember to give the date things are needed by and other important information so that the children have all the information they need. Then arrange for a phone or Skype call to follow up.

Written provocations give real-life contexts for children to be creative, solve problems and develop their own work for a reason; they engender purpose and motivation. The possibilities really are endless, and when used as an infrequent provocational technique it can result in some outstanding work.

Things to think about

- What do you think about the letter provocations?

- Could this be a useful learning device within your classroom and setting?

- Have you seen other teachers using this form of provocation before?

- Have you used this before in your practice?

- Why do you think young children would like this?

- Can you see any areas of the curriculum that this couldn't work in? Why?

Chapter 12

Maths as a Means of Provocation

At this stage I have to admit to a conflict of interest – if you look at the next case study you will see the same surname as mine. Jonathan is my husband and has been a teacher and educator for 30 years (that makes both of us feel really old). I only recently asked him to contribute, and I realise how ridiculous that was – he is the most passionate person regarding maths I have ever met and he sees maths everywhere; which is what we want our children to do. Here is his case study of why maths, as a subject, really is a provocation.

● Provocations in mathematics

Jonathan Longstaffe

School mathematics is a journey; in fact, all of mathematics is a journey from initial questioning into engagement and wonderment and further questions. So how do we, as educationalists, create the environment to foster, stimulate and encourage these questions in children? The questions asked will allow children to become good problem solvers, and this requires teachers to think about how to facilitate children playing mathematically. Playing is important; the opportunity to play with resources and equipment at a young age allows children to experience problem solving at firsthand. Problem solving needs children to ask their own questions, find their own solutions and to realise that actually going wrong in a problem often leads through an iterative process to an eventual solution. To be meaningful to the children, problems need to have some relevance to their stage in life and also don't need to be problems from 'mathsworld'. By mathsworld, I mean questions that appear to be rooted in real life, but really are meaningless for the majority of people. For instance, how many people in their weekly shop buy 40 watermelons? I raised that in a training session once and I was stopped after the session by the person who had just brought the refreshments in and he actually would buy 40 watermelons in one go – he was the catering manager! So how do we create the environment to engage the children? A video message asking for help? A secret message in code? A visit to a museum or art gallery to look at articles that can be used to stimulate the imagination? A series of pictures to fire the imagination?

This picture was taken in the Praça de Dom Pedro IV in Lisbon, Portugal:

- How could this picture be used to stimulate enquiry?

- Could it be projected onto the floor and the children encouraged to describe what they see?

- What questions could be asked by the children about the picture?

  – Is the floor level?

  – Does it go up and down?

- What do you think it would be like to walk/cycle over it?

The children could be encouraged to look at the different shapes in the picture; this could develop into exploring how different shapes fit together, a starting point into tessellations.

How else can children be encouraged to ask questions? How could you carefully set the environment to encourage children to ask questions?

The more children are encouraged to ask and solve their own questions at a young age, the more the children will be good problem solvers as they move through mathematics at school and beyond. The ability to solve problems by thinking creatively is increasingly needed by employers and will continue to be needed for the foreseeable future. Provoking children to ask questions early on will foster this enquiring approach in future years. The more children can play mathematically early on, the more they develop a feel for the questions to ask and have the perseverance to find a solution; these skills will stand them in good stead for the future.

I have a confession to make. When I was at school, my feelings about maths ranged from OK on a good day to 'Why?' on a bad day. My confidence was low and I experienced many unhappy years with teaching that neither stimulated me nor made me curious. I certainly didn't experience the joy of numbers or of discovering how and why shapes tessellated to make patterns. The only time I became interested was during my Art exam classes when a new teacher taught us about drawing optical illusions. If only someone had used that as a provocation when I was younger!

My point is that maths is such a rich and varied subject that provocations can come from so many places, all enabling children to become passionate about a subject that is often something people feel proud to say they are bad at and don't enjoy! If our youngest children can gain that sense of joy and wonder within maths, we are helping them to stop the rot with the negative feeling associated with the subject. The creativity, expression and diversity needs to be reflected within the activities that young children can explore and investigate. Provocations can do this and should be used to enable children to play and explore the concepts before any formal representation is done. Indeed if the formal representation is forced upon children without the concrete understanding, they will continue to experience problems. Through play and exploration we can successfully enable children to make connections, to see patterns and to have the confidence to move forward in all aspects of mathematics.

Small parts provocations are an excellent place to start to build children's understanding and satisfy their natural curiosity. Outdoor play involving nature and observations of natural pattern, shape and colour all contribute to understanding further along the mathematics path. Work within water and sand play, including aspects outlined in other chapters, build children's capacity to make mathematical connections and to draw comparisons. They also provide valuable extended times where small groups of children can explore mathematical vocabulary and engage in discussions where they can share theories and ideas relating to complex mathematical ideas. The play and exploration enable this to happen.

Provocations in maths again demand a large and varied selection of materials and resources. But many of these items will already be in use within a setting and can be utilised in different ways. Collections of metallic, reflective utensils that hold liquids and that pour satisfy many aspects of provocations and maths all at once. Using a message or letter-type scenario to start a maths provocation in the role-play area of a newly developed 'Workshop' can provide many opportunities to explore mathematical content.

Using large-scale shapes and boxes, cases and containers develops children's understanding of shape and space, and crafting up the outdoors develops the understanding of measurements and area.

Maths is such a creative area and has so many connections to art that many provocations can start here: patterns in materials, wallpaper, birthday presents wrapped in paper and ribbon, themes on traditional pottery, tartan, Arabic and Aztec traditional tile prints, and work linked to building design and architecture. Invite a local designer or architect in to talk to the children about their job. Or someone who designs playgrounds. Use this as a provocation to make a new design for somewhere in your locality. See how their imagination grows and works to solve the problem.

Give the children time to explore and 'be' a designer, an architect or a builder using their maths skills. Let them make connections and be mathematicians, and not simply do maths.

Have your resources readily available and ready for children to make connections with. By working in this way they will be more creative and push their boundaries.

Jonathan Longstaffe is the Priority Area Lead for the Advanced Maths Support Programme and works extensively with schools and teachers across the UK. He has been a very successful secondary headteacher and is a published author.

Chapter 13

Tweak the Outdoors!

We are familiar with provocations in the outdoors in ECE. How many of us work in settings with specifically designed and developed outdoor areas? Lots of us have garden areas where we grow and cultivate flowers, plants, vegetables and fruit and use them in other areas of our work, such as cooking, baking, drawing and early science and geography work. We use large outdoor physical play areas, story areas, mud kitchens, workshops and wildlife areas. And how many of us are involved in a weekly or fortnightly Forest School session? A lot, I would guess. The question I want to ask is, how many of us regard these things as a provocation? Some definitely, but some of you reading this book have maybe never considered these invaluable aspects of our practice as provocational in any way.

I'm arguing now that they are and they can be by simple changes of attitude and tweaking. I also believe that by using these, not on a daily basis, but regularly over the course of a two-week planning period, or a month, that a number of the key skills we want to develop and encourage within our children will be developed through regarding and planning with a focus upon provocations. We regularly plan for our children to engage in activities that develop observation, curiosity and investigation, and we want them to be actively involved in developing their reasoning skills and problem solving and in sharing resources. By including the planning aspect 'to provoke', we can make these things real and a central part of the focus of learning, which will enable the children to develop these skills in an exciting and different way.

So here are some examples where things have been 'tweaked to provoke'.

ADD UNFAMILIAR THINGS TO EXISTING FAMILIAR OUTDOOR RESOURCES

The outdoor adventure/physical/climbing play area

How often do we expect children to engage with additional resources within the confines of an outdoor physical/climbing area? If we did, what would happen? Would the children think they needed to be tidied away or would they play with them and integrate them into their climbing and physical explorations?

Leaving a large treasure box or trunk under a partially enclosed aspect of a large outdoor climbing area will automatically engender children's curiosity and they will want to explore what is inside. The box could indeed be filled with 'treasure' or it could be filled with books and book characters that are linked to an area of the curriculum that you are covering at the moment. Leave an unmarked box of mixed construction equipment next to the slide or tunnel area and see what happens and how the children utilise this into their play. Add a box of old cameras that can be used for symbolic play, with a working camera that the children regularly use in sessions, and see how they are provoked and use the resources. Place a container of paper and art materials within the climbing area and discover how the provocation works and motivates the children to explore their art skills and work.

Changes in the 'mud kitchen'

Add role-play clothes or set up a new eating area, including things that can be made into tables and chairs and place settings with enough resources for four or six people. A sealed cardboard box with a range of bubble mixture and bubble wands can be cheaply and easily bought from £1 shops and bargain shops; keep an eye open for when they are available and store until needed. Let the children 'find' a range of missing clothes (some obviously dirty and some clean) to make outfits around the mud kitchen and surrounding outdoor area. What do the children do with them? Include musical instruments in the regular kitchen resources that the children go to use, and include some laminated sheet music and a recording device the children are familiar with; see how the children respond and develop the use of the provocation. Reduce the number of resources you have in the kitchen and only include a small number of items that the children can transfer and pour water with. Follow this up with only having scientific and mathematical measuring jugs, tubes, funnels and items with standard measures marked on them; these resources are more familiar in a Key Stage 2 classroom, but it's never too early to introduce these things in a play-based situation. See what happens and what the children discover from this 'older-age' provocation. In addition to this, add a range of balloons and see how much capacity work goes on during the session.

If you want to dive into a longer mud kitchen provocation that is perfectly suited for the summer term (when hopefully the weather is better), this is the one for you. You will need to enlist the support of your headteacher and other colleagues and it needs to be done when the children are outdoors and actively using the kitchen area. It also relies on you and your colleagues giving a convincing performance in order to set the scene and kick-start the provocation. I call it the 'DIY mud kitchen' provocation. If you've ever watched *DIY SOS*, you'll already have an idea of what I mean. If the children have, then you're already onto a winner, as they will have an idea of the kind of work they might be doing.

Brief your headteacher, as you will be asking them to come out to see you when the mud kitchen is being used and talk to you about how it's looking a bit tatty and 'really needs to be updated'. Ask them to stay as you stop the children and ask them what they think. Start the discussion about what needs to be re-painted, or cleaned, or decorated. At the start of the following day, tell the children that the headteacher has asked the children to organise a *DIY SOS* project for the mud kitchen and that they would like it to be done by the end of term. Tell them that there is some money for the project but that they need to think of other ways to make this happen. At this stage you can decide to include specific suggestions or not. These might include asking parents to help, sending letters to local businesses and companies for help, getting children to visit other classes throughout school and ask for their help and suggestions, making posters and signs to place around school and on school external notice boards to ask for donations, and getting other members of staff to help. This stage is dependent upon how far you want to take this provocation, and the planning is half the fun. It's a little bit like winding up a clockwork toy and letting it go. The first stage is yours, but after the provocational input the rest is dependent upon the children and the way they engage with and develop the provocation and the methods you use to enable the provocation to have legs and run.

'Crafting up' the outdoors

If the children have been previously involved in any outdoor craft activities and projects this can be a very effective provocation after they have experienced a gap between the initial learning experiences and the provocation. Leave a large drawstring sack or bag close to a boundary wall or fence containing a range of string, wool, ribbon, material and coloured templates with lace holes. See if the children's earlier learning impacts upon how they use the materials or adapt them to decorate their environment.

Have a large container of empty boxes, bottles, tubs and tins arrive during the start of the week and leave it in a specific spot outdoors. Make a point of telling the children that it is there. The container should also have a smaller container full of smaller items such as a tub of small stones, beads and twigs. Also include string, wool, sticky-tape and chalk so that the things can be adapted and attached to other items by the children. What will they make? Make a pile of large and oversized sticks, elastic bands, wool, string, strips of material and large coloured drapes and/or sheets. Leave them for the children and other adults to discover at the start of the week. See how the children respond to the resources and see how they use the things that have been left. If they are regular explorers in Forest School, you may get camps, tents or dens; or they may design and produce something completely unexpected.

Note: We obviously need to be very safety conscious when children are involved in challenging, physical play that can involve heights, slides and steps. Complete risk assessments are a must, and close observation and monitoring will ensure all children are safe.

A LONGER-TERM OUTDOOR PROVOCATION: THE FAIRY GARDEN SCENARIO

At this stage we know that many children and lots of settings creatively use the outdoors and utilise the strength of these areas for the good of the children. The power of the outdoors and the benefits that it can bring are well known, and we only have to look to the numerous mentions of health and wellbeing related to fresh air and being outside to know how valuable outdoor learning and early years gardens really are. Many children experience planting seeds or bulbs to grow spring and summer flowers, and those fortunate enough to have larger garden plots will plant vegetables and use these in other learning activities such as making soup, salads, sandwiches and more. These learning activities are always very carefully planned and directed in order for the children to learn the most from them and to ensure their learning outcomes are met. However, with this provocation I am advocating the exact opposite of this. I think the perfect provocation will show you, as a practitioner, what the children know about growing and will provide the children with an opportunity to display leadership skills, cooperation, planning, organisation and speaking and listening skills. It will also include key maths and number vocabulary and will go on to develop into a long-term caring project for the children.

Resources

- A wheelbarrow – empty to start (or a large container)

- Compost/topsoil

- Watering can(s)

- Trowels

- A range of plants (these can be seasonal)

- Gardening gloves

- Some additional decorative resources to be used – shells/stones/leaves

- Hand sanitiser suitable for children

- Caps and sun hats to be used if sunny or hot

- A letter or card from the fairies/pixies addressed to the children in your class

- The provocation outlined for the children in the card or letter, sent from the fairies or pixies:

> Saranja and Rennikk had saved up to make a special wheelbarrow garden. They had saved their pocket money and birthday money; they had done jobs and asked if they could have plant cuttings from their favourite neighbour, who loves gardening. They had got everything together and were so happy. They left the plants, wheelbarrow, soil, trowel, gloves and watering cans at the bottom of their garden so that they could start the next day. When they woke up and went into the garden, everything had gone! It had been stolen and they were devastated. They didn't know what to do and who could help. Then they saw the children playing in their school garden and thought that they might be able to help them. Saranja and Rennikk wondered if the children would be kind and help them by rebuilding their garden.

Note: Ensure children have all used sun cream if required due to the weather conditions.

So the scene for the provocation has been set; the children are involved and have a very special job to do. You can decide to leave all the resources readily available for the children to find and use when they arrive one morning or you can add another element of 'discovery' and problem solving by having some of the resources readily available for the children and others that they need to search for. If you have a storage area for gardening materials, they could find the soil and watering cans there; perhaps the plants may be in another space in your setting and the children may need to go to borrow some things from other classes when they realise they need them (gloves, trowels, etc.).

Now, I'm certainly not saying that a provocation should not be planned; quite the opposite in fact. What I am saying is that the planning for a provocation is different from planning in a usual context. The above information gives the basic overall outline and the resources list provides a guide for the resources you can use. This can and should be adapted to your particular needs and setting.

The format of the letter (as discussed in Chapter 11) is a means of passing on instructions and guidance to the children and is one of the first parts of a provocation of this kind. Along with the resources and the setting up that will be carried out by the practitioners involved, the letter starts the active involvement of the children and sets the scene for the provocation. As the teacher or early years practitioner, you should be fully immersed in the role of receiving the letter (giving some background to the children such as where it was left, when you found it, etc.) and reading and sharing it with the children. This is the part of the provocation that links to the practice of 'teacher in role', making sure the imagined situation feels genuine and that the children can in fact fulfil the role that is being asked of them.

The next stage is supporting the children as they move into their role to fulfil the things that have been asked via the letter. During this stage the role of the teacher is to act as enabler and facilitator, to observe what the children do and to step in to teach things that need to be taught during the provocation. It also provides you with an excellent opportunity for observation and assessment of what the children already understand and can demonstrate.

Your role might be to:

- demonstrate how to plant a flower

- demonstrate how to water the plants when the garden has been planted

- model the vocabulary and language related to the provocation

- ask questions, including open-ended ones for moving the learning forward throughout

- observe the children's responses and roles they play

- assess the children during the provocation and use this to plan the next stages in their learning.

Remember, the provocation is part of the continuous provision, a planned context for effective teaching and learning and one that helps to create a stimulating learning environment. The provocation within the continuous provision element of any planning also relates directly to our understanding of child development and how and why our youngest children learn. We also need to consider and plan for the children's 'now-interests' – the things that are motivating them now and the things that you have observed are fascinating them as the year and terms progress. This is where the environment and outdoor play come into their own. As the year and seasons progress, children can actively experience the rapid, awe-inspiring changes that the natural world can bring. These concrete, real-life experiences also reinforce the children's longer-term learning and long-term retrieval. As Tom Sherrington said:

> expos[ing] children to real, concrete examples so that they can then remember these and relate to more abstract concepts... results in deeper understanding and minimising misconceptions. (Tom Sherrington 2019)

It's lovely that, as a secondary headteacher, Tom knows and understands the value of these experiences and is spreading the word via education social media, his blog posts and his writing.

This really is music to my ears and I'm sure to so many early years teachers and practitioners. We know and understand the power of concrete play and practical investigations and explorations as children move from the Foundation Stage into Year 1 and above. It is wonderful to see this being promoted and reinforced by secondary schools and colleagues. Concrete development is so important to everything that children do in order to consolidate their understanding and learning. They need to be able to repeat and further explore things, and this is where learning through outdoor provision and provocations meet.

Longer-term provocations really depend upon having a creative mind and in acting as an artful educator, where everything is viewed as a potential for learning. It is being open to what can provoke an interest, curiosity and passion in the children and also within yourself, as you, after all, are the person who has thought of the initial idea. It might be a theme you want to add to planning meetings at the start of a new term or academic year and you might want to start a list of ideas that could be used in the future.

Things to think about

- Would you like to 'tweak the outdoors'?

- Could you see yourself using any of the above ideas?

- Do you know of any other practitioners that you would like to share these ideas with? Are any of them working in your setting?

- How often do you change the resources in your mud kitchen?

- Have you ever used some 'unrelated' items as a provocation for your outdoor areas?

- How do you think your children would react to having a selection of role-play clothes 'hidden' under the climbing area? Do you think your children would integrate them into their play without asking an adult for permission first?

- Do you see 'crafting up' the outdoors as something that could support your children's gross and fine motor skills?

- Could you begin to compile a list of resources that you could use for longer-term provocations?

- Could you develop a plan for initiating and developing professional discussions around provocations in your setting? Can you decide how they could be used successfully in your setting?

- Whether you could go to observe a longer-term provocation in a setting close to you.

- What benefits and long-term learning could be achieved through utilising these forms of provocations?

Chapter 14

Be a Magpie!

I am so fortunate in my job. I get to work with lots of different schools and so many wonderful early years staff who are passionate about providing the very best opportunities for the children in their settings. Whenever I am holding a course or delivering a training session, I ask people about visits to other settings: how often they go to visit other early years staff, if they are part of a larger early years or ECE network, if they encourage people to visit and share with them. I know exactly where this love of visits came from. As a young, inexperienced teacher, I was fortunate enough to get a job in the most wonderful infant school, where I worked with a group of exceptional teachers. They taught me so much and offered continuous, daily and weekly continuous professional development for me through their encouragement, professional reflective discussions, guidance and enthusiasm for teaching our youngest children. They met each and every situation with total professionalism, open minds and great understanding; particularly when faced with children's behavioural difficulties and related issues. Everything was brought back to child development, where the child was at that particular time, and what we needed to do to support them and advance their understanding and learning.

I was also given a mentor as part of my first year who quite simply inspired me to be the teacher I became and am today. I am also fortunate to say that we became great friends and she continues to inspire me to this day. She understood the value of seeing other settings, classrooms and types of schools and organised me to make local visits as part of my ongoing development. She also introduced me to a local network of after-school twilight sessions where I made connections with countless people at countless schools. I learned so many things as a result of attending these meetings. Their present-day equivalent is probably the Teach-Meet sessions that are organised throughout the country and the BrewEd meetings that have become so popular in the last two years. There really is a grassroots movement of teachers who are passionate about sharing the things that are going on in their classrooms and schools and being massive supports for other professionals they make contact with.

So I am a great advocate for visiting other people and seeing their settings and of course their children. Every time I go to a new school, or somewhere I haven't been for a while, I get butterflies as I know I'm going to see something I love, and that makes me smile. A visit is a brilliant way to re-energise your practice, to be inspired and, let's be honest, a cheap way of getting some Continuing Professional Development (CPD)! Here are just some of the reasons why I love visiting other teachers in their own settings. Oh, and I adore the idea of being a magpie and picking up all of those sparkly ideas.

REASONS FOR VISITING OTHER SETTINGS

- Be a magpie and see or 'pick up' so many ideas and things
- Pick up ideas relating to organisation, structure, routine, behaviour strategies, discussions with children, questioning, working with colleagues
- Collect display ideas
- Investigate how others use their indoor and outdoor space

- Develop your understanding of a new areas, e.g. Forest Schools/P4C
- Build up resource ideas
- Observe how the classroom environment is organised
- Study the way staff talk to children and build relationships
- See how a different behaviour policy operates
- Learn about the reading development, the immersion in books and reading
- Build an understanding of transition from YR to Y1 and beyond
- See how staff teams work together and how specialist higher level teaching assistants/teaching assistants are deployed
- Observe systems and routines
- Find out about family involvement/parent partnerships in schools
- See how other teachers build home–school links
- Learn about community links and development projects
- Find out about specific aspects of learning and curriculum approaches
- Make connections with other professionals
- Build up an early years network
- Be an early years 'listening ear' or 'buddy'
- Organise regular early years 'Teach-Meets'
- Hold them in a different setting
- Start the journey again by being a magpie there

It has been during some of my visits to other settings and schools that I have seen and talked to colleagues about the provocations they have used. Some I have already mentioned, and they have been included in the case studies throughout the book. Others are included below. As you can see, being a magpie certainly pays off!

● Case study: Play and the outdoors

Michael Follett

Have you ever watched *Ready Steady Cook*? If not, the premise is that cooking contestants are given a big kitchen to use and a cupboard and fridge with a range of surprise ingredients. In the allotted time they need to come up with the best dishes they can using those ingredients. Play and cookery have a lot in common. I am a playful cook. I prefer to muck about with what's in the kitchen than follow recipes. Sometimes it works and occasionally it is horrible.

There are three elements to a great play environment:

- Culture – beliefs, values and principles

- Fixed environment – the landscape, topography, spaces and equipment

- Ingredients – movable, transformable, combinable material

CULTURE

The culture of play means you must understand and value the play process and must be resilient to hurt and dirt. In my kitchen I accept I may get hurt. I have fire and knives and scissors, gas and glass. If I am going to cook I have to accept that I may get hurt and I will probably get messy. I am prepared to put up with this because I love to cook and I find the process and creativity rewarding.

If a play setting's culture is not resilient to hurt and dirt and if it only provides entertainment and adult-devised activity, or demands predetermined outcomes, it cannot also deliver the full range of benefits of play.

FIXED ENVIRONMENT

In my analogy the fixed environment is the kitchen – the cooker, fridge, etc. Many early years and school settings only focus on the fixed outdoor play environment and when designing their provision are happy to outsource its content to a play company to install fixed play equipment. This may or may not have much value to it, depending on the design's ability to continue to provide challenge to children. However, it can only ever be the kitchen, providing the fixed, unmovable furniture of play, and nothing more.

INGREDIENTS

In this case study I want to talk about the third element usually referred to in playwork as 'loose parts'. They form the play equivalent to cooking ingredients. They are there to be mixed, combined and concocted into whatever the child's imagination desires.

Throughout history, for as long as children have played they have commandeered any resources they can find around themselves to supplement and enrich their play. Children will play in, on and with anything they find in their environment. When play was a process that most children had freedom to experience without adult intervention, there was little need for a theoretical understanding or a policy-based approach to the provision of playable materials. In the past children were able to find the times and the resources to fuel their play. But childhood has changed, and in developed countries, children have lost the time, spaces, permissions and resources which allow and enrich their play experiences. If we value the process of play in children's lives, and if we accept that good play opportunities are a right and necessity of a childhood, then we need to be purposeful and informed in our approach to all aspects of provision of play.

In order to understand why loose parts are particularly effective in supporting play, we need to relate their function to definitions of play. The playwork sector in the UK has three commonly agreed principles describing the play process. They are that play is freely chosen by the child, is for the child's own intrinsic motivations and is directed by the child. In my playwork practice I regard these as the 'Playworkers' Compass'. I might need to navigate away from them; I may have to place restrictions, or provide some direction, but I should always question why, and I should return to their direction as soon as possible.

In my book *Creating Excellence in Primary School Playtimes* (Follett 2016), I also describe play as the process of creation of experience for the sake of making sense or 'framing' that experience. Intelligent learning is the result of creatively interpreting self-generated data. In their play, children create experience, exploring the realms of physical, mental, social and cultural actions. As their actions produce feedback from the real world, children 'frame' or allocate increasingly sophisticated levels of interpretation and meaning to the raw data they have generated. The meaning of play lies in the role of the child in the creation and framing of the experiences they themselves have initiated and created. The essential condition is that the child is the agent of all three stages of experience, first the creative initiator, then the self-directing actor and finally the interpreter. This cycle is often referred to as 'agency', a term which refers to the child being the person who acts on their own behalf behind all three stages in the cycle.

When children are still babies, we take the concept of agency for granted. Nobody gives their baby walking lessons because they know that the only way to learn to walk is to keep doing it until you can. It is not an externally informed or logic-based learning process; it is driven by a natural developmental instinct, develops through self-initiated attempts and improves by tiny incremental adjustments made by the body and the brain. The child is the agent in the process; they have the urge to walk, they experiment with each step and they make the adjustments needed based on their direct firsthand or primary experience. Observation of the way that we see children learn through experimentation and reaction should tell us that this process is valuable and therefore we should provide them with enriched environments where the potential for many, many different self-directed actions is possible.

This is where the theory of loose parts comes in. In his paper 'Why we should stop cheating children' (1974), landscape architect Simon Nicholson proposed that for every additional movable, combinable resource made available to children in a play landscape there is an exponential increase in the potential possibilities or play value of that environment. We can imagine that a child playing in an empty concrete square has far fewer possibilities for play and discovery than a child in a concrete square with a tyre, a plank and a traffic cone. We can gain a better understanding of why this is if we link Nicholson's theory to Hughes' Taxonomy of Play Types (2002). Hughes categorised children's play into 16 different recognisable types. Each of these is linked to the way children explore the relationship between the four realms of experience: self, material realm, social realm and cultural realm.

If we take any one of the play types, we can see that the addition of plentiful, open-ended loose parts into the play environment is going to greatly increase children's ability to explore that type of play. For instance, in *symbolic play*, children learn to assign symbolic roles and characteristics to objects that are different from those presented by the object. In our example the traffic cone might become a passenger, the tyre a cloud and the plank an aeroplane or a boat or a crocodile. These symbols do not have to be based on the qualities of the object. To support symbolic play we only need to provide objects; children can be left to assign their own symbolism to them.

Another play type is *object play* where children explore the qualities and nature of an object by playing with it. In symbolic play a saucepan can represent anything; object play is much more practical as the child uses the object for their self-directed purposes. A saucepan may be used in object play as a receptacle, a bat, a hat or a step-up. An essential requirement for object play is lots of different objects to play with. A condition in object play is that children are free from adult preconceptions of what an object is for and how it is used.

In *socio-dramatic play* children act out or perform a narrative of a social situation or role, in an imitation-of-life performance. This kind of play is greatly enhanced by props. These may trigger the play; for example, a briefcase may trigger an episode of play around going to work or a hard hat about being a builder. A rich and eclectic source of loose parts will undoubtedly enrich socio-dramatic play.

There are 16 play types: symbolic, locomotor, recapulative, creative, exploratory, communication, socio-dramatic, role, fantasy, deep, object, mastery, rough and tumble, dramatic, social and imaginative. If we look in depth at each of these play types we could see how the addition of plentiful loose parts would fuel and stimulate a much wider and richer variety of play within the type.

Many early years practitioners learn to view the complexity and developmental value of play through the concept of schemata. These are common organisational concepts which children are driven to investigate, and Piaget (1936) saw them as one of the essential elements in children's cognitive development and the building blocks of intelligence. A schema can be used to describe any pattern of behaviour that helps us catagorise and make sense of the world. In play and early child development the commonly accepted schemata are: rotation, trajectory, enveloping, orientation, positioning, enclosure/containing, transporting and transformation. The investigation of any of these schemata is only possible within an enriched, open-ended environment, where time is allowed for experimentation, practice and engagement. The process is only meaningful because the child is exploring their relationship with the world, understanding the influence of their actions and driven by their own motivations. Limited schematic play can take place in the relationship between child and environment. In exploring a trajectory schema, the child may explore their movement up, over, around and between the fixed environment, but the possibilities of this two-way relationship are limited. With the addition of a movable object, a triangular relationship opens up between child, environment and object. When multiple objects and materials are present, the potential to explore schemata expands into almost infinite possibility.

It is a common misconception that because much play takes place in the imagination then physical resources are not needed. We would not think that an imaginative artist did not need paints, or an imaginative cook, ingredients. Each object has its own qualities of weight, texture, size, colour and its properties to be playfully explored. Its movability means that it can be taken anywhere in the fixed landscape and the child can explore how each object relates to each of the four realms of experience:

- Me and my body (self)

- Physical environment (material)

- Other people (social)

- Cultural context (culture)

A cardboard tube, for instance, might be put over my arms to make them stiff and straight (self), I can roll it down a hill (material), I can whisper through it to my friend's ear (social) and I can pretend it is the stethoscope of a doctor (culture).

When children play in an environment full of loose parts, they are explorers and inventors in ways that they cannot be in a fixed environment, and the true value of loose parts comes with quantity. Nicholson points out that they provide an exponential increase in possibilities for each thing we add. Loose parts can start to relate to each other by being placed in, on or alongside, in a multitude of positional and imaginative relationships. This 'combinatory play' (Bruner 1957) requires the formation of new ideas, innovative thought, experimentation, predication and conceptualisation. These qualities all require the child to be at the start and heart of the play process and its progression, and unsurprisingly are all characteristics of intelligence.

One reason loose parts are so valuable is because they don't have a fixed function or purpose. Some items such as an old suitcase may appear to, but in the playful environment it is permissible for it to be used in any way a child wishes. Adults may see it as a case, but a child may assign it to symbolically represent absolutely anything or they may want to investigate its possible functions, as a container, a platform or a form of transport.

Playworkers have a further concept that is relevant in deepening our understanding of why loose parts are especially valuable: 'adulteration'. This is the understanding that just by being adults and being present near play, we have an impact on it, and as we increase our proximity to play, we increase the likelihood that we are disrupting the child-centredness of the play process. When we actively start to intervene in the play process, we are most likely to 'adulterate' it, because it will be less directed by the chid, chosen by the child for the child's own internal motivations, and more imprinted by the adult's desires and influences, whether intentional or not.

Good loose parts are robust and/or have little or no monetary value. A cardboard box is not robust but has no monetary value and is easily replaced. If a child chooses to squash it, sit in it, put water in it or collect things in it requires no intervention from the adult, allowing the play process to flow 'unadulterated'. A tyre requires more work to source but is incredibly robust and has little or no monetary value. The child can incorporate the tyre into their play however they like, and the resource does not require adult intervention to prevent misuse or damage. This reduces the adult's perception that they need to intervene to protect the play resources or ensure that they are being played with in the right way, and so there is less adulteration of the flow of the play process.

The lack of the need to prescribe a 'right way' to play with loose parts increases their play value but does not relieve the playworker of their role in providing a safe enough environment for children. The playworker is responsible for the kind of objects that are made available in their play environment and should exercise judgement in the kind of loose parts made available, their condition and how they are being used. In making these judgements the concepts of risk and hazards are useful. If an object presents a strong possibility of injury without benefit, and if the cause of harm is not apparent or predictable to children, we can think of it as being a hazard.

Hazards

A broken bottle in long grass, for example, does not have play benefit and cannot be easily identified or predicted by the child. We can remove the broken bottle and the play value of the environment has not been diminished. A nail sticking out the back of a wooded pallet is not visible and predictable and can be removed without diminishing the play value of the pallet.

Risks

Providing rocks to play with does give the possibility of injury, but there are many benefits to playing with rocks. They are cheap, have attractive material qualities, and have many uses supporting many of the play types and schematic play. The potential injury from rocks is apparent and predictable by children.

One of the difficulties in assessing whether loose parts are safe enough to include in the play environment is the idea of intent. No object is dangerous on its own, only in how people interact with it. Sadly, many school playgrounds provide nothing at all to play with, because at some point in history a child has used an object with malicious intent and so the object was deemed to be at fault and removed. There cannot be a hard rule about intent. Adults need to know their children and think about what they are likely to do with the stuff they give them, but they should base their decision making on normal and reasonable behaviour and not on the worst possible scenario. We can use the example of rocks again. Rocks do not throw themselves around and so are not inherently dangerous. During normal behaviour we would not expect children to throw rocks at each other, and if they did, a reasonable response should be to teach them not to. Rocks are not dangerous, but throwing rocks is dangerous; we will therefore need to assess the children for their social and self-control skills and support them to not endanger themselves or each other, rather than deny them the many benefits of natural or fabricated loose parts play.

In addition to the provision of loose parts, schools and settings should plan carefully how children will access them. Following play theory by maximising the child's role and minimising the adult's, we want as little adult intervention between the materials and the children as possible. They should not be stored in sheds or shelves which require adults to choose and access them. Fabricated loose parts storage should be accessible and simple for children to find, select and put away. Storage should be wide, not narrow, have as much door width as possible, not have high shelves that require adults to access them, and only have a minimal degree of sorting and separation. Natural loose parts should form part of the 'found environment'. They are best in a wild garden where rocks, logs, bark, branches, sand, stones and water are scattered and accessible to be found and used as children play.

Anywhere in any good play environment there should be abundant natural and fabricated loose and open-ended materials for children to draw into and enrich their play.

Michael Follett BA PGCE is Director of OPAL Outdoor Play and Learning and the author of *Creating Excellence in Primary School Playtimes* (Follett 2016).

Things to think about

- How do you feel about being a 'magpie'?

- Do you have opportunities to visit other settings and magpie ideas?

- Are you part of an early years network, either informally or formally?

- Would being a member of an early years group or network help you in your work?

- Could this contribute to your CPD?

- Where do you get your best ideas from?

- How would you feel about opening up your classroom for others?

- Would you consider hosting a Teach-Meet session for early years staff?

- Are you a member of an online education network?

- Has this helped your practice?

- Would you recommend this to other colleagues?

Chapter 15

The Power of Your Community

The importance of supporting things going on in your locality and using these events throughout your year to stimulate provocations cannot be overestimated. Events that are near to hand and can also be supported by families and parents and friends are vital in developing strong community links and in creating strong learning opportunities that are unique to your setting. It really is a win-win situation.

In my locality we are very lucky as my home town is known as a 'festival town' and we have numerous events that schools can become involved in and use as a provocational stimulus on a monthly basis. We are also surrounded by a large number of local groups that are keen to become involved in community work and support local schools. But I am well aware that some places are not that lucky and do not have so many amazing opportunities right upon their doorstep. However, please don't let that stop you accessing local events, beginning with researching them and bringing them to the planning table to discuss and see if they are of any use within your curriculum and as a stimulus for your provocations.

As I mentioned in the last chapter, I am a bit of a magpie, and whenever I go into different schools and settings I actively look out for things that will spark my imagination and give me a 'oh, OK, wow' moment. I also advise people I work with to adopt the same policy and basically be cheeky and make a concerted effort to be open and aware to other possibilities. We all need inspiration to help and support us in our planning and to provoke those 'wow moments' in us so that we can do the same for our youngest children. Schools are super-busy places and we can all become bound up with our own little bubbles. It's at these times that we forget to look up and see the amazing possibilities that exist everywhere if we only take time to look.

I also make sure that I'm aware of all the local things that are taking place in my locality and also a little further afield. These can spark some fantastic provocations and link beautifully to longer-term planning that may link to work being done in other year groups and across the school as a whole. We all know that things are usually planned around 'big events' such as international sporting events – the World Cup, Olympics, etc. – and things like a Royal Wedding, but what about planning some whole-school events that focus upon your locality? Maybe you have an annual charity event or a tradition that is not widely known about. These things can have a tremendous impact upon children's learning, teamwork and overall wellbeing.

Here are the local things that have been used by early years staff for themes and provocations in my area. There will definitely be similarities in your area but differences as well.

Our autumn festivals and events start in September, and the biggest event of the year is arguably our Lantern Festival which has been taking place as part of our Market Charter festivities since the 1990s. It is a real community event with workshops taking place during the late summer and early weeks in September as children and families make large lanterns with wicker withies, covering them in special paper and adding decorations and eventually lights so that they create a river of lights that are carried throughout the streets, and eventually meet and travel to a huge celebration and fireworks at the end of the evening. Each year has a new theme; in the past these have included Under the Sea, Houses and Homes, Transport, Cartoon Characters, Films… Lanterns are also made in workshops in local schools, and school groups lead the part of the procession to the middle of the town centre. The whole event can be used as a provocation for learning or as an initial introduction to the yearly theme and moved on from there. In the late autumn we have a Dickensian Festival which is a wonderful provocation to use to develop early historical skills and to use as a start to the Christmas period. Provocations can be built around historical clothing, artefacts, stories or role play.

In the spring we have a flag fortnight where each shop and business in the town centre displays a brightly coloured silk flag from the front of their premises depicting their business. The bookshop has books on the flag, the cinema has an old-fashioned film roll and the bakers bread and cakes, all unique and all telling a visual story. Flags as a basis for a provocation are a delight and can be linked to kites, weather, design, making, drawing and painting. I know a number of settings that have based work around flags and flag design during this time of the year.

During the following months there are walking festivals, retro revivals, comedy and music festivals, including an international music festival, Print Fest and a huge number of country fairs; all with things to excite and motivate the children and provoke their learning and discovery.

We are also very fortunate in that we have an international Buddhist Temple within five minutes of the town and so schools are able to use this as a truly wonderful stimulus and provocation for learning. Just a visit to the grounds is enough to make children wonder and ask questions. Visits there are a thing of peace, grace and beauty. So many learning possibilities can take place from experiencing a firsthand learning experience of that quality.

I am also close to the coast and to the Lake District and so these areas are also rich sources of inspiration and are frequently used to develop and enhance the curriculum whether through Forest Schools, day visits, themed weeks or longer work.

My unique location is special, but your location will be too. It is the ultimate resource – use it to its full potential.

Things to think about

- How much does your community and community involvement influence your planning and teaching?

- Do you use community events as a stimulus or a form of provocation for your children?

- Do they have regular opportunities to become immersed in local culture and events, thus building cultural capital?

- Could you invite members of your local community into your setting to support your work or as part of a larger-scale provocation?

- If you are already involved in some aspects of community life, could this be extended and further developed to support learning through provocations?

- Would the parents and carers like to be involved in this process to support their children's development and learning?

Chapter 16

Provocations of Visitors and Visits Out of School

Throughout my career I have been a huge believer in the power of visitors to school and in taking children and young people out of school to visit rich cultural, historical, religious and socially important places. I touched on this in the previous chapter. All these experiences can and do play a major role in developing children's understanding of so many things. This is particularly true when you live and work in an isolated or remote community. If you haven't got access to certain things on your doorstep, I truly believe you must make the effort to search these places out and provide rich, provocational experiences that build real understanding in so many ways. The provocation is implicit in these situations: a person who inspires comes into your school, your classroom, and makes you realise anything is possible; a visit to a new town or a city when you have never experienced that before; or a trip to the seaside and a coastal town for the first time. These are life-changing experiences with the power to transport children's understanding and broaden their horizons.

The brilliant Mick Waters, in his book *Thinking Allowed on Schooling* (Waters 2013), talks of the need for a better definition of what 'rounded education' is and for reducing the inequalities children face. His chapter on experience of learning is excellent, with some wonderful examples of schools where children experience the basics of art, dance, drama, music, learning outside the classroom, mending and making things, growing, cooking, making scientific, geographical and historical discoveries, meeting and discussing with people in a different first language, and linking these powerful experiences to all aspects of literacy and mathematics.

There are so many wonderful opportunities for visitors to come into a school setting and turn a usual day into something extraordinary. Looking at these days from a child's point of view can help us to see how special these experiences really are and can then lead us to explore the possibilities that can take place after someone new has started a provocation. From visits by a local police officer, dentist, pet shop owner, vet or author to setting up video chats to people across the globe, in classrooms thousands of miles away, or even on the European Space Station, visitors are an exceptional way of starting a provocation. Children can run with ideas after a visit, and learning can be developed in numerous ways and directions.

Visits to places outside of the school setting also have the same effects and cannot be overestimated. In terms of cultural capital, these visits can be a crucial part of a longer-term plan to develop children's knowledge and understanding and can offer firsthand experiences that cannot be explored in a school building. Possibilities could include a local or regional museum, gallery, theatre, sporting venue, unique place of interest and a special event. Each visit can form development over a half term and can have far-reaching learning opportunities that children will remember and talk about for many months.

The important thing is being aware of what is happening locally and how you can utilise it.

Chapter 17

Twitter, Pinterest and Instagram

The Power of Social Media

If, like me, you need to be able to find information and inspiration quickly, some of the greatest free resources can be found via social media. I know at times it takes a terrible bashing from a whole range of people, but whenever I go to schools, or deliver courses, I recommend that people take a look at Twitter, Pinterest and Instagram if they haven't already done so. A number of teachers can be a little reluctant, but personally it has freed up a great deal of time for me and has enabled me to make some wonderful links with fellow professionals throughout the UK, in Europe and across the world. I must admit I wouldn't be without it, and although it can feel as if you can disappear down the rabbit hole for a while, it frequently brings more positives than negatives; and spending a while down the rabbit hole can also be a joy. You only need to find that one little bit of magic and you've won the day. I am also good at tuning out the negative people who tend to shout too loud. If they aren't providing a feed I feel is valuable then I unfollow and don't worry about it. After all, it's just like a technology-based book, but with more characters; if you weren't enjoying a book, you would just close it and put it down. I do the same thing with social media. If you are sceptical, the following are my personal rules for school social media use.

- Remember you are using this for your profession – be professional at all times and be aware that everything can be traced back to you, even if you think it can't!

- Think before you post and follow school and professional association guidelines – check them out if you haven't already done so, they're really helpful.

- Be selective about which platforms you use and explore.

- If you set up an account, keep it for work only and be clear about what you want from it.

- If you know you can get 'sucked into' trawling through information, use the strategy of setting a timer on your phone and stick to it; you'll then be more productive.

- The ability to follow inspirational people, become involved in discussions with other professionals and to save ideas that you can use later is a joy. The connectivity is a huge bonus when time is precious.

- If I see an idea that I would like to use, I always send a message to ask if that's OK. I've found people to be incredibly generous. In fact this book is a result of the connections I have made via Twitter.

- I've personally found Twitter and Pinterest of most use for EYFS ideas and inspiration.

- The early years social media community is a thriving and enthusiastic place. It can help to feel that sense of community and shared interest and purpose. Social media can help you to feel that you are part of a much larger EYFS community.

- A section of further resources is included later in the book. I'd love it if you took a look and it helped you on your way.

I first met James via Twitter and our like-minded approach to education and school. We are both passionate advocates of creativity in learning and in the urgent need to re-evaluate the present education system that many of our children still find themselves in which dates back to the 1950s. His work with the Educational Collaborative for International Schools (ECIS) is very closely linked to the key skills recognised by the World Economic Forum, Andreas Schleicher and Sir Ken Robinson. Here is what James has to say about things:

● Case study: The importance of 'soft skills'
'ROBOTS ARE COMING FOR THE JOBS'
James Wren

If indeed the 'robots are coming for the jobs', then never before has it been more vital for these skills to be a priority and 'put right up there'. A good friend of mine is Creative Director for a large global advertising agency in New York. We recently talked about education and what it was that he looked for when graduates arrived for interview at his company. He told me that he'd seen the very best CVs coming from students with incredible grades from top-notch universities, but, often, these were not the people he wanted to hire or hired. He would say to candidates, 'Tell me about yourself', and they would automatically rattle off their grades. 'No, stop there, stop telling me about your grades, tell me where you want to go.'

He was frequently met with a blank stare and silence.

The point is, when it comes to school, the vast majority of time is spent preparing to be tested, and then after tests are taken, the letters or numbers obtained are put on the CV which determines (in the eyes of the system) how intelligent an applicant is. However, when we do research and look at where the shortage is, it's not the academics, but the soft skills we need, and which people like my friend are increasingly interested in during the recruitment process.

Watch the trailer on YouTube for the 'Most Likely to Succeed' documentary and you will see exactly what I mean. It's not about creating corporate worker bees, quite the opposite in fact. It's about an education system for now and the future that encourages creativity, free thinking, ideas, tenacity, collaboration and intrinsic motivation.

James Wren is brand designer for the Educational Collaborative for International Schools (ECIS). He has previously taught communication design at international schools and worked for a number of design agencies. He has also run workshops focused upon idea generation at schools around the world. He is passionate about the development of the creative curriculum and students taking the lead in their own learning. He is an experienced voice artist and a published author.

TOP 10 THINGS FOR SIMPLE ADULT/ TEACHER PROVOCATIONS

- Dress up – wear something different!
- Act in role
- Sing what you do! Yes, really!
- Paint spots on your face
- Wear a hat
- Whisper for the day
- Write, don't speak!
- Bring in your pet (have a pet day)
- Eat your lunch with the children
- Get really messy

 **Things to think about**

- What are your feelings about social media as an educational network?

- Are you a member of EduTwitter, Pinterest or Instagram?

- What benefits have you experienced from being a member of these groups if you are?

- Would you consider trialling them to see if they could support your work in the early years?

- Can you share your ideas in other ways?

- How do you feel about the development of 'soft skills' and are they a part of your regular practice within your setting?

- Why are soft skills so important for now and for the future?

- Do you actively plan and develop these skills in your setting and with your children?

Chapter 18

Using Provocations in Learning with Older Children

Furness Future Leaders Academy Project

I know you might be thinking 'What has provocations in learning with older children got to do with early years?', but I think it's important to show how this way of working can and does work as children move through school. In its simplest form it's about grabbing someone's attention and sparking an interest. It's also about keeping that interest going. I've spent quite a lot of time outlining the reasons for using a strategy like provocations and why they are important for children both as they are working within them and for the attributes and skills they engender in them for the future. That's why longer-term provocations and related projects are important – they continue to build the skills the young people will need in their future lives and in their future work. We all need to be aware of that.

Furness Future Leaders Academy (FFLA) is a shared project that takes place each summer with children in Year 5 and is sponsored by local industries and organisations. It has a number of external partners and aims to develop key skills within the children who attend the programme that will enable them to have successful careers in the future. One key skill is leadership; others include confidence, trust, creativity, adaptability, collaboration, teamwork, prioritising, organising, presenting and campaigning. The programme has been in existence for the past five years and has used research and development skills to provoke learning and understanding within the students, securing long-term growth and development within schools and communities. FFLA has successfully utilised residential opportunities to extend research and analysis-based work, including scrutiny of data and preparation, resulting in powerful student presentations that were made to community and industry leaders. The programme is a very powerful provocational tool indeed and has had tremendous results with long-term gains being recorded by students, parents and schools.

The work of the FFLA aims to inspire young people to plan their own future and take an active role in working together across school groups to develop the skills that will help them to achieve a bright future. One key element of the programme itself is the following provocation: the students need to plan and carry out a successful campaign based upon a topical national or international issue. They will be responsible for all aspects of the campaign: deciding on the subject of the campaign itself, coming up with a name and logo, deciding who will take which role and carry out key responsibilities, holding press interviews, leafleting members of the public, working with adults in key positions from partner agencies, and producing a detailed presentation that will take place at the end of the project. They will do all of this as part of a new partnership group, working alongside students from other schools that they do not know. Collaboration, creativity, initiative, emotional intelligence, teamwork, critical thinking and analysis, problem solving, leadership and determination are key, as well as humour, listening and cooperating. All of these qualities have been noted by World Economic Forum leaders in their future jobs survey 2018. These students are working on future skills development now. They really will be ahead of the game and developing the very things they need for their future.

This is not the only project of this kind taking place. Some are in the planning stage and others are well established; many of them base their work around a key provocation that grabs the students' attention, keeps interest and motivation high and places them in a position to actively rehearse and develop the skills they will need for their future, in which they will have numerous roles and more than one career. They will, in all likelihood, be involved in jobs that have not yet become a reality. These students will need to react and respond in a way that we never have. We need to make sure that they are ready for this. The use of these projects and the use of similar provocational projects within schools will provide a jumping-off point for students; we need to ensure that they are a regular feature so that these key 21st century skills become a reality for our children.

TOP 10 THINGS TO DO IF YOU WANT TO DEVELOP A LONGER-TERM PROVOCATION

- Liaise with other schools and colleagues to build a project
- Contact local industries and businesses for support
- Link with local secondary schools and further education colleges
- Contact local education charities for support
- See if your local MP can help
- Investigate funding streams
- Seek support from parents and carers
- Use the local press to publicise your ideas and gain support
- Use local radio and social media
- Ask the children to write, email and contact organisations – the personal touch works!

 **Things to think about**

- What are your thoughts about FFLA?

- Do you see the value in longer multi-agency projects for young people such as FFLA?

- Do longer multi-school and industry-linked projects take place in your community?

- Would you like to be involved in a project of this type?

- What do you think the benefits would be as a teacher and educator?

- What do you think the students' views would be and why?

Some further things to think about:

- Do you think children need to have been involved in provocations when they are younger in order for them to be effective learners in a project like FFLA?

- What do you think are the benefits of being involved in a long-term intensive provocation such as FFLA?

- Do you and your children have access to any long-term projects of this kind?

- Can you see any issues or problems with long-term provocations?

- Why would you like to be involved in a provocation such as FFLA?

- Have any of the longer-term or permanent provocations inspired you?

- Do you have any ideas for the future after learning about the work of other teachers and practitioners?

Chapter 19

To Finish Where We Started

A PERSONAL STORY: POETRY, PROVOCATIONS, PASSIONATE WRITERS AND FRIENDS FOR LIFE

The one thing that has always motivated me as a teacher, educator and now a writer is finding those things that really make me and the children and professionals I work with tick. Those things that grab you, excite you and make a difference to your way of working and thinking. And in my experience these can also be things that surprise you and are not always positive. Negative or challenging things can certainly bring out the very best in you! And in the children!

A few years ago I was searching for something that would 'set alight' an upcoming poetry unit and I was determined not to fall back into familiar materials, poets and poems. I had started to plan about a half term ahead as I really wanted to get this right. I had a fantastic mixed-age Key Stage 1 class of boys who were very enthusiastic and made up of a wide range of different characters, abilities and passions. I had always included planned elements of things that the children liked, enjoyed and had a real interest in, and at the time we were having a whole school push on developing high-quality cross-curricular writing. Added to this we had some idiosyncratic parental views regarding what boys should be doing regarding reading and writing. I woke up early one morning during the Easter holidays and realised that if I was clever and brave enough to meet this head on I might be able to break down some stereotypical views that some parents held, work with the children to produce some outstanding writing and do some positive public relations by publishing the poems and getting the books out to the parents and the community. So, win-win! All I had to do was find the right poetry to cover this and I'd be home and dry. Really it wasn't a lot to ask!

I've always loved the process of pre-planning, organising resources, collecting things, scouring what I already have and then trawling through libraries, charity shops and all sorts of places, including galleries, exhibits and museums, that might bring some inspiration and add to my resources. My Easter break was spent gathering ideas. I always initially use a large-scale drawn plan to help me to clarify my ideas, not quite a flow chart or a spider diagram, but a combination. During the planning stage, with lots of drawing, colour coding (with colour pens of course – I am an early years teacher through and through!) and jottings, I realised that a theme was emerging. We were due to cover environmental and locality-based work in Geography and I thought it would be a great idea to combine the two and actively build as many links and connections as possible. As a school we had been involved in a number of very successful environmental projects and had a strong Eco School Group as well as a national Healthy Schools Award and green awards from our local council. It was all coming together. I was also very aware of the fact that, if I could match the work we were doing to the very specific geographical and social area that the school was in, we could also move towards changing some of the idiosyncratic and very traditional views that were held by some people and that were being passed on to their children. If someone were to ask me what my overarching aim for the unit of work was, I would have said 'to develop and create thoughtful, creative, expansive writers' and to actively support the boys in really viewing themselves as writers. At this stage I began to realise that what I really needed was poetry that was rooted in reality, that wasn't remote or old, but was from now, was fresh and was relatable to the children in my class and in my school. These boys had to see a real, understandable reason not only for writing, but for writing poetry; something that, if we were being absolutely honest, they and the people in their families couldn't see the reason for at the moment.

I drew up (another!) list:

- Recent up-to-date poems

- Written by boys/men

- Environmental focus

- Countryside/outdoor location

- Not old fashioned!

- Must be good, great words

- Motivational

- Demand to be re-read

When I looked through the list, and my initial planning, I thought it would be a minor miracle if I was able to find something. I remember having a long, animated discussion with my husband about it and he laughed at me and said when had anything like that ever stopped me. Over the years we've often had that conversation.

So I decided to look at any new resources that were being produced locally that might fit with my brief. Local community-based work or charities proved to be fruitless and there were no events or exhibitions that were taking place around the time of the planned unit that I could tag on to and enrich the writing experience for the children through a visit. I really wanted to make this as rich and rewarding as possible. A long-time motivator for whatever I was doing was to make memories for the children. I had a nagging feeling that this was something I needed to pursue. Whatever I planned needed to fulfil this; it had to be meaningful and make memories alongside the poetry. It seemed to be niggling away at the back of my mind and I was determined to make this an unforgettable writing project for the children.

I knew I had the luxury of time but I was also conscious of the need to find my main source material. I decided to look through recently published poetry books and anthologies, young writers' collections and work related to conservation and environmental issues. I dismissed using anything that was over five years old and recognised that this would seriously limit my resources, but I felt it had to be relevant and show that poetry wasn't just something that was consigned to the past and had been written by people that were now all dead – harsh but true! If my boys were to see the relevance of the unit, and a reason for writing poetry, it had to be about something that mattered to them and that they could see the logic and motivation in.

I spent a lot of fruitless hours searching education websites, author sites and publishing sites for any kind of inspiration. I did find some modern poems that were about the countryside and animals that I decided I could use as a way in and as an initial introduction if I didn't find what I wanted. I also wrote some truly awful attempts myself and rejected them immediately. I knew my limitations! The clock was ticking. I needed inspiration, and fast.

My mum always used to say that nothing was impossible. I'd talked to her about what I was doing and she was, as always, an eternal optimist and had 100 per cent faith in me and the fact that I would find that special thing that I was looking for. 'Just keep going, it'll find you when you least expect it,' she said. She was right, as always. It did find me and it was when I was least expecting it. In fact I found just what I wanted via a website that had no real connections to what I was looking for. The only real connection was that it was a site with a connection to words and music and that was, for me, inspirational. The moral of the story is, be aware of everything.

This is what happened.

On the website was a tiny piece about a community poetry book. If you didn't scroll right to the end of the site you wouldn't have seen it. It didn't give a lot of information, but it did say the book had been written as a response to a council building project where a number of ancient trees and wooded areas had been demolished in order to build a new road. I was intrigued; this tiny piece of information provoked me and provoked a huge sense of needing to know within me. Could this be the very thing I had been looking for? Would it be the thing I needed to base my unit of work upon and would it help to break down some of the barriers that existed in my traditional locality? I ordered a copy and waited. I had nothing to lose and so much more to gain. If nothing else I had another book to add to my collection and I'd supported a charity along the way, as all money from the sale of the book was donated to Cancer Research UK. This really was a provocation in action. What I couldn't have known at that point was how much of a provocational tool this would be. Not only for me as a teacher and educator, but also for my children and for the work that we created that half term and over the following two or more years. It also provoked a massive personal change in me as a person as I was fortunate enough to make a lifelong friend as a result of reading that tiny piece at the bottom of a webpage and through sending for that book. When the parcel arrived it contained a copy of the poetry book and a thank you letter. I sat and read every poem immediately and knew within half an hour that this book was just what I had been looking for. It successfully ticked off everything on my list and then added to the things I could plan for in such a beautiful way that I knew the work would be a success. I sent for a further four copies as I knew other people would find the book as inspirational as I did.

The book captured the passion and desire local, everyday people felt about their beautiful locality and heritage being snatched from them and destroyed. It was simply produced, but powerful and beautiful in equal measures. It was real and relevant and was forged in a community of people who cared passionately about their rural location and the unique environment they lived alongside. The quality of writing illustrated the frustration they felt in response to the immovable officialdom of the council and the devastation they felt when all their efforts went to waste and the bulldozers rolled roughshod across ancient sacred ground, ultimately destroying 200+-year-old trees. Their pain was tangible, and the impact it had on my class was quite simply immeasurable. What it did do was release a unique symbiosis that linked the people who had experienced and written the poems and my children who lived in a very similar environment where the land and its ancient heritage was part of their everyday lives. Geographical distances melted away and the words provoked and inspired writing of a level I have very rarely experienced as a teacher. Children who had previously shied away from any form of creative writing were not only hugely motivated, asking when we were writing again and bringing in beautifully constructed poems that they had written in their free time, but were more motivated in other areas of their work and using their increased range of vocabulary throughout the curriculum too.

The poetry book, and the poems within it, formed a provocational platform from which I was able to successfully cover each aspect of the objectives that I had originally outlined. We compared our unique locality and the locality related to the poetry book, finding similarities and differences that extended way beyond the curriculum guidelines for Years 1 and 2. We explored each poem and became involved in wide-ranging explorative discussions covering every aspect of the National Literacy Strategy outlines and the National Curriculum for poetry. Challenging and exciting vocabulary became the norm and it became a daily competition to use the most effective and dynamic words you could across every lesson, not just in literacy lessons.

Our environmental and geographical work also took a dramatic turn and children were able to see the reasons behind the work we were doing. They became passionately aware of the roles they played in preserving the environment and in ensuring that detrimental practices did not take place in their corner of the world. They were a living embodiment of what a high-quality provocation can do within the classroom and how it can be used to transform children's learning. As for writing, it bloomed and blossomed in a way I could never have hoped for. Children using writing techniques and structure that were years beyond their actual age became a regular occurrence and they wrote boldly and without fear or constraint. They had been inspired by people who had turned to poetry to explore and express their feelings about the destruction of their treasured environment and my class were desperate to produce poetry that replicated the same feelings and emotions when they wrote about their own environment.

The summer term became the things that teachers dream of. Every literacy session was met with absolute delight, and subsequent lessons were filled with questions of 'When can we write more poems?' and 'Do you want to see what I've written?' and loud, excited discussions about new words and ways of putting them together. My biggest problem was stopping them writing! What a brilliant problem to have.

This poetical provocation didn't finish when the summer holidays arrived. As I had a mixed-age Year 1 and 2 class, I had the lovely privilege of having my Year 1s as Year 2s. What I couldn't have expected was that they were just as passionate about poetry and their writing as they had been at the end of the previous year. My challenge was how best to respond to it.

I was met by my Year 1s (now Year 2s) who were still 'in love' with poetry and writing. I could solve some of this by including poetry in story sessions and lots of choice in the reading areas and on book displays. However, this wasn't enough for them. They wanted to see if there were more poems that hadn't been used in the collection. They decided that they wanted to write to the people who had written the poems and see if they could answer their questions. So the provocations went on. What followed was something I have never seen or experienced before or since. Yes, I'd been involved in times when children had really taken a theme or idea and ran with it, when they had asked to correspond with people, writing letters and passing on stories, but this took on a life of its own. It also made me prouder than I have ever been about anything in my career. These children passed on their passion for writing, words, poetry and letters seamlessly to the new Year 1 children who had moved into our class from Reception. Within a matter of days the enthusiasm and spark for writing both in classes and outside of school had seemed to flow between both age groups, and after one weekend I was met by pages and pages of writing that children had done at home and who were desperate to share with the rest of the class when they got back to school. I cannot take credit for what happened next, I was simply open to it and realised that this was a unique learning situation and I could either go enthusiastically with it and be a facilitator for the experiences or I could shut it down and carry on with what was planned. As a good early years teacher, I went with the children's passions and interests, something I will never regret.

I know I was lucky that when this took place I was a very experienced class teacher, who had specialised in Literacy for a number of years, and I was a confident professional who had always been passionate about creating exciting learning opportunities for all my children. I was also a senior leader, and this gave me the self-confidence to understand and know what the children wanted and to use their ideas to plan the next stages of the learning.

The class decided to write letters to the person who had compiled the poems and produced the book. I hoped that they might get a reply, but as with a lot of these things people are busy and not everyone thinks of writing back to a group of five-, six- and seven-year-olds.

The first letter arrived less than a week after I posted the request asking if there were more poems. And with it came a little bit of magic that continued to support the children's writing process and gave them an insight into the world of words, stories, books and emotional literacy that I could never have dreamed of. My class had unknowingly opened up a dialogue with someone who was as passionate about writing, stories and the environment as they were. It was the perfect partnership, and with every letter and exchange the relationship and friendship grew. The writing became fluent and expansive. The children turned from young beginner writers to confident, expressive writers who understood the reasons for written communication and connections that only a letter in the post can bring. What was becoming apparent was that the books and guidelines that state 'use real-life situations' didn't just mean use them as examples. What makes the most startling and developmental difference is when children have an extended period of writing for real-life purposes, as my children were experiencing. Then the need to use full sentences, accurate punctuation and spelling and interesting and descriptive words means something. They were experiencing this every few weeks as the letters went back and forth. We started saving the letters we received for the end of a morning session, and the intensity in which the children listened to what their 'writing partner' had to say was a pure pleasure to share.

The children continued to write beautiful, explorative poems that demanded to be read. A few of the older children asked if we could put them into our own book and see if we could get it published. A wonderful colleague, who was just as passionate about writing, was more than happy to help with this and organised a beautiful anthology that was used to raise funds for our school library. The initial provocation continued to gain ground, as when my children were asked to write in other subjects they would ask if they could write a poem. Poetry was at the heart of everything they did; boys and girls equally used the medium to express many ideas and had no reservations about doing so. This made for a language-rich environment where words were king.

You might think that is where it ended, with a regular exchange of letters and poems. This was really only the start. When the children started writing to their 'writing partner', they had no idea that she was not just a poet but an author who was writing a book. Over the next year we got regular packages which would always contain a lovely, thoughtful and funny letter and then slowly the letter would be joined by pages and then chapters of a newly written book – a gentle, beautiful story with a dog as its main character. The children clamoured to hear what happened next to their favourite dog and wrote back enthusiastic letters full of questions and ideas. We realised that the chapters we were receiving were the first draft of the book and we were the first people to read it; we built an understanding of how a book was produced, edited and published. All of this as a result of my initial provocation.

The highlight was when a smaller, tightly bundled package arrived one day. As I opened it, in front of the children at the end of another busy morning session, we saw it was a first edition copy of the story, a story the children all felt involved in, invested in and part of. The children were part of the development and process of producing a book. It meant such a lot to them and made so many other aspects of the curriculum real and tangible for them. It continued to motivate them as writers and readers for years and they continued to write and produce poetry books for their 'writing partner' on a regular basis. This extended to letters and cards at Christmas and Easter and when school finished each summer. They had found connections in shared experiences and in a love of words. I'm sure they still have it. As for me, I was fortunate enough to make a friend for life, someone who became a hugely important part of my life and who continues to inspire me to this day. I will be forever grateful. And all this from a provocation.

I can't guarantee that if you use provocations in your teaching that you will have the same kind of experience I had, or that the children in my class experienced. What I can guarantee is that you will be challenged, excited and motivated, you will develop key, much-needed, skills in the children you teach and that you will enjoy the shared experience. I'd love to think you'll have a go. Why not give it a try, who knows where it will lead?

I'm still regularly in touch with other writers who were initially involved in the poetry book that started the whole, rather wonderful learning journey that we went on. I have recently received another beautiful poetry anthology of very personal, touching poems that explore another aspect of one poet's work. I haven't used this with children yet, but I do intend to in the future, if and when the right time comes and I know that it would work with adults and teachers too.

So, the connections keep growing, and the tentacles of the initial explorative search provide a permanent, deep-rooted connection. They keep provoking me in my work and inspiring me to do more. When I have a bad day, or when things are difficult, I remind myself of the lifelong connections, friendships and inspiration that happened as a result of simply searching for some inspiration and something to provoke learning in a class. I know I was fortunate to experience it; I hope you are too. The joy the book brought with it will remain with me forever.

And Finally…

I'm often guilty of falling down the rabbit hole of education social media, particularly Twitter and Pinterest. There is so much inspiration to be found and so many wonderful, dedicated people who are happy to share their ideas and thoughts. It really is a brilliant way to join a larger education community. I particularly like the 'light-bringers', the people who, as Roald Dahl would say, are 'an enthusiast in life', the teachers, leaders and educators who believe 'lukewarm is no good'. I know I can go there on any given day, or night, or at 5 o'clock in the morning for the #teachers5oclockclub with the brilliant Paul Garvey, @PaulGarvey4.

I know that I can share in discussions, ideas and find support and challenge. I can find experts and subject specialists who I would never have access to without social media and EduTwitter. Without my involvement on Twitter I would never have made contact with Andrew James at Jessica Kingsley Publishers and he would never have asked me to consider writing an early years book. I simply would not be where I am now. I'd like to thank those people who help me despite not knowing it and all the other people who have helped and inspired me along the way – people who I have discussed this with, driven mad with my 'what-ifs' and rambled to over coffee. You have all been amazing; especially my husband Jonathan. And particular thanks to Emma, I realised late in the day that I was probably writing this for you. And finally, my lifelong friend and soulmate, who sadly isn't with us any more; you continue to inspire me and motivate me every day, thank you for being a bright star in my life and in the lives of the children we both taught through your poetry, letters and books.

Finally, let's return to the thoughts of Sir Ken Robinson. He argues:

> To realise our true creative potential – in our organisations, in our schools and in our communities – we need to think differently about ourselves and to act differently towards each other. We must learn to be creative. (Robinson 2017, p.240)

Further Resources

RESOURCES AND RESOURCE SITES

There are numerous early years organisations, websites and resources. TTS is probably the best and most comprehensive.

@TTS_EarlyYears
www.tts-group.co.uk/earlyyears

PEOPLE TO FOLLOW ON TWITTER

There are so many fantastic people on Twitter who will regularly share ideas, concepts and things that they have done in their settings. Here are some of the people who inspire me and who you may find interesting to follow:

Nicky Clements – Deputy Headteacher, Head of Early Years
@nickyclements71

Sue Cowley – author, speaker, teacher educator
@Sue_Cowley

CREC – Centre for Research in Early Childhood
@_CREC

Jan Dubiel – independent early years advisor, consultant, trainer and writer
@jan-dubiel

Early Excellence – The Leading Voice of Early Years Education
@EarlyExcellence

EY_Matters – For all Early Years Professionals to Connect, Communicate, Collaborate and Create
@EY_Matters

Flakefleet Primary School – The happiest primary school 2018
@flakefleet

Michael Follett – Founder and Director of OPAL outdoor play
@OPALoutdoorplay

Pam Jarvis – chartered psychologist, author, educator
@Dr_Pam_Jarvis

KEYU – Keep Early Years Unique – writer and campaigner for early years 0-7 years, founder of KEYU
@Keep_EYs_Unique

More Than A Score – If you believe children shouldn't be tested at 4 years of age
@MoreThanScore

Real Play Coalition – Believe in the Power of Play
@official_rpc

Kym Scott – early years consultant, trainer, conference speaker
@kymscott5

Kathryn Solly – early years specialist speaker, consultant, trainer and author
@SollyKathryn

Ruth Swailes – school improvement advisor, education consultant, founding member of Firm Foundations
@SwailesRuth

Tim Taylor – author and teacher educator, delivers Mantle of the Expert
@imagineinquiry

Nikki Walters – Head of Regional Development-North of England, Wales & Scotland Early Excellence
@NikkiWaltersEEX

@watchmegrow_Di
@EA_Holmes
@RaeSnape
@oakwoodEY
@BreamoreSchool
@Bransgoreschool
@smithsmm
@IamLauraHenry
@NurseryWorld
@Blue-Coat-Play
@NicolaBurke16
@HYWEL_ROBERTS
@debraKidd
@musicmind

@LittlForestFolk
@helenjwc
@AndyBurtEEX

PINTEREST

If you want to find some instant inspiration for your classroom, displays, provocations and anything else early years related, try Pinterest. So many early years practitioners use it as a quick and simple way of sharing ideas and things that they have been working on.

RESEARCHERS

If you are interested in educational research and how this will support and develop your work, the place to go is:

The Chartered College of Teaching
@CharteredColl
https://chartered.college

This is the professional body for teachers and educators. It provides a wide range of research documentation and professional development meetings and courses.

The British Association for Early Childhood Education is also another excellent place to go for early years support and information, again offering professional development opportunities and conferences.

The British Association for Early Childhood Education (Early Education)
@earlyed_uk

Other great resources include:

The Centre for Research in Early Childhood
@_CREC
www.crec.co.uk
@earlyed_uk

Professional Association for Childcare and Early Years (PACEY)
@PACEYchildcare

British Early Childhood Education Research Association
BECERA Association
@BECERAASSOC

European Early Childhood Education Research Journal
@EECERJ

Early Childhood Research Centre, University of Roehampton
@ur_ecrc

National Day Nurseries Association
@NDNAtalk

READING AND BOOK LINKS INCLUDING ORGANISATIONS

SAPERE
@SAPERE-P4C (UK's national charity supporting P4C)

Book Trust
@Booktrust

The Reading Agency
@readingagency

Reading Rocks
@readingrocks
https://wherereadingrocks.com

Carnegie Greenaway
@CILIPCKG

World Book Day UK
@WorldBookDayUK

Faber Children's
@FaberChildrens

Chicken House
@chickenhousebooks

PLACES TO VISIT

Early Excellence is a specialist national centre dedicated to Early Years and Key Stage 1 pedagogy. It has a highly interactive environment where practitioners can go to be inspired. Early Excellence offers specialist support, training and advice for schools and they have an outstanding classroom setting and resource shop to support your practice.

Early Excellence Huddersfield
@EarlyExcellence
www.earlyexcellence.com

Many schools are delighted to be contacted by early years professionals who wish to make a visit to their setting. I have mentioned a number throughout the book.

EVENTS TO ATTEND

Nursery World Show, with two national exhibitions each year, one taking place in London and one in Manchester. See:

@nurserywrldshow
www.nurseryworldshow.com

Early Excellence National Conference
www.earlyexcellence.com

The Cambridgeshire Festival of Education
@CambsEdFest
www.cambsedfest.com

Books to support provocations

From Ordinary to Extraordinary – The Curiosity Approach
Lyndsey Hellyn and Stephanie Bennett (2019)
Publisher: The Curiosity Approach

Looking for Learning: Provocations
Laura England (2019)
Publisher: Featherstone

Child Centred Planning in the Early Years Foundation Stage
Jo McEvoy and Samantha McMahon (2019)
Publisher: Learning Matters

Learning Threads for the EYFS: Practical Activities for 3–5 Year Olds
Eleanor Hoskins (2019)
Publisher: Learning Matters

Schemas: A Practical Handbook
Laura England (2018)
Publisher: Featherstone

The Nursery Year in Action: Following children's interests through the year
Anna Ephgrave (2015)
Publisher: Routledge

Loose Parts: Inspiring Play in Young Children
Lisa Daly and Miriam Beloglovsky (2014)
Publisher: Redleaf Press

Princesses, Dragons and Helicopter Stories
Trisha Lee (2015)
Publisher: Routledge

A Child's Work: The Importance of Fantasy Play
Vivian Gussin Paley (2005)
Publisher: University of Chicago Press

The Boy Who Would Be a Helicopter: The Uses of Storytelling in the Classroom
Vivian Gussin Paley (1991)
Publisher: Harvard University Press

References

Bruner, J.S. (2006) *In Search of Pedagogy, Volume 1, The Selected Works of Jerome Bruner, 1957–1978*. London: Routledge.

Children's Commissioner (2019) 'Early access to mental health support.' Available at https://www.childrenscommissioner.gov.uk/wp-content/uploads/2019/04/Early-access-to-mental-health-support-April-2019.pdf, accessed on 19 April 2019.

Cowley, S. (2017) *The Artful Educator*. Carmarthen, Wales: Crown House Publishing.

Department for Digital, Culture, Media & Sport and the Rt Hon Jeremy Wright (2018) 'Britain's creative industries break the £100 billion barrier' [Press release]. Available at https://www.gov.uk/government/news/britains-creative-industries-break-the-100-billion-barrier, accessed 2 November 2019.

Department for Education (2007a) *The Early Years Foundation Stage: Statutory Framework for the Early Years Foundation Stage and Guidance for the Early Years Foundation Stage*. DfES. Available at www.standards.dcsf.gov.uk/eyfs, accessed on 19 April 2019.

Dubiel, J. (2019, July 10) *Love this... Glastonbury recreated in playground*, 10/7 [Twitter post]. Available at https://twitter.com/jan_dubiel/status/1149028710567337984, accessed on 17 January 2020.

Fearn, H. (2019) 'Busting the "intent" myth.' Ofsted. Available at https://educationinspection.blog.gov.uk/2019/07/01/busting-the-intent-myth, accessed on 17 January 2020.

Fisher, R. (1990) *Teaching Children to Think*. Cheltenham: Nelson Thornes Ltd.

Follett, M. (2017) *Creating Excellence in Primary School Playtimes: How to Make 20% of the School Day 100% Better*. London: Jessica Kingsley Publishers.

Gussin Paley, V. (2008) Keynote speech, Wonderplay Early Childhood Learning Conference. Available at https://youtu.be/wWxYRkmHNXM?list=PLDN_6TK_-dNY3-g-amMEgjMeWqGbJFNYH, accessed 21 November 2019.

Heathcote, D. (1984) *Collective Writings on Education and Drama*. London: Heinmann Educational Publishers.

Hughes, B. (2002) *A Playworker's Taxonomy of Play Types*, Second Edition. Ely: Play Education.

James, C. (2015) *The Garden Classroom*. Boston, MA: Shambhala Publications.

Kasriel, S. (2019) 'What the next 20 years will mean for jobs – and how to prepare.' *World Economic Forum Annual Meeting*. Available at https://www.weforum.org/agenda/2019/01/jobs-of-next-20-years-how-to-prepare, accessed on 19 April 2019.

Leach, P. (2010) *Your Baby and Child*. Dorling Kindersley: London.

Ma, J. (2018) 'The Future of Education.' World Economic Forum Annual Meeting 2018. Davos-Klosters, Switzerland. 26 January 2018.

Malaguzzi, L. (1998) 'History, Ideas, and Basic Philosophy: An Interview with Lella Gandini.' In C. Edwards, L. Gandini and G. Forman (eds) *The Hundred Languages of Children: Reggio Emilia Approach*, Second Edition. Westport, CT: Ablex Publishing.
Miller, E. and Almon, J. (2009) *Crisis in the Kindergarten: Why Children Need to Play in School*. College Park, MD: Alliance for Childhood.
Montessori, M. (1967) *The Absorbent Mind*. New York: Holt, Rinehart and Winston.
Nicholson, S. (1971) 'How Not to Cheat Children: The Theory of Loose Parts.' *Landscape Architecture 62*, 30–35.
Ofsted (2019a) *The Education Inspection Framework*. Available at https://assets.publishing.service.gov.uk/government/uploads/system/uploads/attachment_data/file/801429/Education_inspection_framework.pdf, accessed 17 October 2019.
Ofsted (2019b) *Ofsted's new inspection arrangements to focus on curriculum, behaviour and development* [Press release]. Available at https://www.gov.uk/government/news/ofsteds-new-inspection-arrangements-to-focus-on-curriculum-behaviour-and-development, accessed on 7 May 2019.
Ofsted (2019c) 'Ofsted's blog: The new education inspection framework' [blog post]. Available at https://www.tes.com/blog/ofsteds-blog-new-education-inspection-framework, accessed on 17 January 2020.
Piaget, J. (1936) *Origins of Intelligence in the Child*. London: Routledge & Kegan Paul.
Pierson, R.F. (2013) 'Every kid needs a champion' [Video file]. Available at https://www.ted.com/talks/rita_pierson_every_kid_needs_a_champion, accessed on 19 April 2019.
Pritchard, E-L. (2018) 'The mental health benefits of going for a walk can last for 7 hours, according to pioneering new study.' *Country Living*. Available at https://www.countryliving.com/uk/wellbeing/news/a180/mental-health-benefits-nature-outdoors-study, accessed on 7 May 2019.
Real Play Coalition (2018) *Value of Play Report*. Available at https://www.realplaycoalition.com/wp-content/uploads/2018/11/The-Real-Play-Coalition_Value-of-Play-Report.pdf, accessed 21 November 2019.
Robinson, K. (2006) 'Do Schools Kill Creativity?' [Video file]. Available at http://ted.com/talks/sir_ken_robinson_do_schools_kill_creativity, accessed on 22 March 2019.
Robinson, K. (2017) *Out of Our Minds: The Power of Being Creative*, 3rd edition. Hoboken, NJ: John Wiley & Sons.
Schleicher, A. (2019) 'Fireside Chat: 21st century learning' [Presentation]. London: Learn It Conference.
Tan, S. (2007) *The Arrival*. London: Hodder Children's Books.
Waters, M. (2013) *Thinking Allowed on Schooling*. Carmarthen: Independent Thinking Press.
Sherrington, T. (2019, February 10) 'Curriculum Notes #1: Start out real, concrete, authentic' [Blog post]. Available at https://teacherhead.com/2019/02/10/curriculum-notes-1-start-out-real-concrete-authentic, accessed on 19 June 2019.
Ward Thompson, C., Aspinal, P. and Montarzino, A. (2008) 'The childhood factor: Adult visits to green places and the significance of childhood experiences.' *Environment and Behaviour 40*, 1, 111–143. DOI: 1177/0013916507300119.
World Economic Forum (2018) 'The Future of Jobs Report 2018.' *Centre for the New Economy and Society*. Available at http://www3.weforum.org/docs/WEF_Future_of_Jobs_2018.pdf, accessed on 19 April 2019.
Yogman, M., Garner, A., Hutchinson, J., Hirsh-Pasek, K. *et al.* (2018) 'The power of play: a pediatric role in enhancing development in young children.' *Pediatrics 142*, 3. Available at http://pediatrics.aappublications.org/content/142/3/e20182058, accessed 21 November 2019.

Index